THE

"There's Jack Nicholson . . .
and there's the rest of us."
Robin Williams

"If I were in trouble,
I could count on Jack.
I mean, *truly* count on—
not hear the famous Warren Beatty,
'Can I get back to you?' "
Peter Fonda

"He makes me feel like
I'm surrounded by about
eighty people when I'm with him.
Ambushed!"
Meryl Streep

"Jack will never do a scene
the same way twice—even when he's
been brilliant the first time."
Harvey Keitel

"I discovered how much
room there is
in the back of a Daimler."
Margaret Trudeau

"My life has gotten better
as I've gotten older."
Jack Nicholson

Other Avon Books by
Barbara Siegel & Scott Siegel

THE ENCYCLOPEDIA OF HOLLYWOOD

JACK
NICHOLSON

THE
UNAUTHORIZED
BIOGRAPHY

BARBARA SIEGEL

AND

SCOTT SIEGEL

AVON BOOKS ◆ NEW YORK

This book was originally published in the United Kingdom/Australia in 1990.

AVON BOOKS
A division of
The Hearst Corporation
105 Madison Avenue
New York, New York 10016

First Avon Books Printing: April 1991

AVON TRADEMARK REG. U.S. PAT. OFF. AND IN OTHER COUNTRIES, MARCA REGISTRADA, HECHO EN U.S.A.

Printed in the U.S.A.

RA 10 9 8 7 6 5 4 3 2 1

For Steve Bornstein—

We met when we were eight years old.
We may have changed,
but the friendship that binds us never will.

ACKNOWLEDGMENTS

The authors wish to express their deep gratitude and appreciation to our English editor, Valerie Hudson, with whom it has been a distinct pleasure to work. Her perceptive editorial judgment and nerves of steel in the face of tight deadlines are most impressive.

We are also grateful to our American editor, Chris Miller, who has carefully guided this book into its new and updated edition.

Special thanks must also go to Ken Englade, a talented writer and thoughtful friend, who helped get this project rolling.

Finally, there are a great many people who have either worked with or who have written about Jack Nicholson, and we are indebted to them all. Their recollections, interviews, and reportage have helped us come to a fuller understanding of a fascinating man.

JACK NICHOLSON

THE
UNAUTHORIZED
BIOGRAPHY

CONTENTS

INTRODUCTION

AT THE END of the 1980s, actor/comedian Robin Williams described the Hollywood pecking order as "Jack Nicholson, and then there's the rest of us." Top-billed in *Batman,* the highest-grossing movie in motion picture history, Nicholson has managed that rare accomplishment of combining near unanimous critical acceptance with huge personal popularity. His mercurial performance as the Joker in that film was the culmination of more than thirty years of acting experience, as well as more than fifty years of wildly adventurous living.

In the pages that follow, you will read about a man who has led an extraordinary existence. Born under mysterious circumstances, he was raised under a cloud of well-meaning falsehoods. Later, he did the unthinkable, turning his back on a college scholarship to run off to Hollywood. Once he began acting, he gave himself ten years to become a star. A little over a decade later, reality seemed to have come up short of his dream. He was getting ready to give up acting and to work behind the camera when stardom suddenly, unexpectedly, beckoned, thanks to his highly praised performance in the surprise hit of 1969, *Easy Rider.*

His body of work since then is full of many of the cinema's most outstanding movies and most electrifying performances. He spoke for an alienated generation in *Five Easy Pieces* (1970), plumbed our sexual psyches in *Carnal Knowledge* (1971), explored the dark recesses of the human soul in *Chinatown* (1974), showed us two sides of insanity in *One Flew Over the Cuckoo's Nest* (1975) and *The Shining* (1980), and let us see the devil's handiwork in *The Witches of Eastwick* (1987).

1

From the bleak drama of *Ironweed* (1987) to the inspired action/comedy of *Batman* (1989), Nicholson has consistently, consciously, gone after roles that are different from anything he has played before. For that matter, even when filming individual scenes, he refuses to repeat himself. As actor Harvey Keitel noted, "Jack will never do a scene the same way twice, even when he's been brilliant the first time."

As varied and rich as his professional life has been, Nicholson's personal escapades have been even more amazing. "I've been at parties where Jack's been there, Warren's [Beatty] been there, Clint Eastwood's been there, Bob Redford. All the girls go to Jack," said producer Bob Evans. Nicholson's reputation as a lady's man is legendary in Hollywood. He has been involved or linked with such luminaries as Michelle Phillips, Candice Bergen, Faye Dunaway, Veruschka, and even Meryl Streep. But his steady girlfriend from 1973 to 1990 was actress Anjelica Huston. Not so steady, though, that she didn't leave him for a highly publicized fling with actor Ryan O'Neal, or that he would resist a heralded affair with an English actress who later told (and showed) all in a *Playboy* article and pictorial. Then there's also the case of the child he recently fathered with yet another woman. Of course, Nicholson has never claimed that monogamy was a virtue.

He has had press attention for reasons other than his sexual escapades. Early in his career he was outspoken about his drug use. He told reporter Rosemary Breslin, "I've never resisted my image. I'm the moron who started it. I was honest. I talked about drugs. Then it was, 'Oh, poor Jack, he's a drug addict.' And if you have a point of view, not everyone's going to agree with it. But some of the things that people said hurt me. I'm vibrant, but not a wild man. I even mope a lot of the time. I'm one of those people who asks, 'Am I boring you?' "

Nicholson may be many things, but none of them are boring. A good many of them, however, are not well-known to the public. For instance, he quietly established a scholarship in his name at the USC film school. He also has never turned his back on his friends. He keeps up with many of the same people he knew before *Easy Rider* changed his life. He has even kept the same agent since his prefame days. Within the Hollywood community, Nicholson's reputation for personal loyalty is best summed up by Peter Fonda, who said, "I know that if I were in a trouble situation, I could count on Jack. I mean truly count on, not hear the famous Warren Beatty 'Can I get back to you?' "

Nicholson's public persona, however, has a good deal more of the rascal in it. He understands what most movie fans know instinctively: "There are no mistakes, no movie stars who are bad." With his arched eyebrows, "killer smile" ("My good friend [Diana] Vreeland hung that one of me," said Nicholson), ever-present shades, and charismatic personality, he has kept his fans constantly entertained, whether on or off the screen.

"My life has always gotten better as I've gotten older," Nicholson told *People* magazine way back in 1980. It's more true now than ever. From his beginnings in Neptune City, New Jersey, to his latest triumph in *Batman* and the controversies surrounding the recently released *The Two Jakes,* this book is a chronicle of that remarkable life.

CHAPTER 1

In a Family Way

JACK NICHOLSON IS a risk taker, an experience junkie, a high flier in the world of personal dramatics. He has put his career on the line with seemingly suicidal film choices, openly dabbled in drugs, and has been one of the great skirt chasers (and catchers) in modern Hollywood history. His life is a testament to living on the edge. But of all the incredible events in his more than fifty-four years, the most startling of all occurred without his knowledge. In fact, it took him thirty-eight years to learn the truth: that his closest family members had conducted an elaborate charade to keep him—and the rest of the world—from learning that he was born out of wedlock, that he was an illegitimate child . . . a bastard.

Nicholson was born April 22, 1937, in Neptune City, New Jersey, a small, backwater town not far from the honky-tonk summer resort city of Asbury Park. His mother's name was June. She was seventeen years old and unmarried at his birth. It was a scandal in the making. Both young June and little Jack's lives would have been ruined in that far more conservative time. Something had to be done, and Jack's grandmother, Ethel May Nicholson, did it. She claimed that the child was her own, fathered by her none-too-dependable husband, John.

John Nicholson, the erstwhile papa, acquiesced to the plan, but he didn't stick around very long. He was an alcoholic window dresser and sometime sign painter who abandoned the family not long after Jack's birth. He was known to drift back into their lives from time to time, usually around Christmas. Nicholson later recalled, "I . . . never really had a relationship of any significant longevity with my father. He was rarely around. He was an incredible drinker. I used to go to bars with him as a child and I would drink eighteen sarsaparillas while he'd have thirty-five shots of Three Star Hennessey. But I never heard him raise his voice; I never saw anybody be angry with him, not even my mother. He was just a quiet, melancholy, tragic figure—a very soft man."

Ethel May was not soft. Not a bit. She held the rest of her family together with sheer grit and determination. June was the oldest, followed by fourteen-year-old Lorraine, and then the infant, Jack. In order to keep food on the table for her kids, Ethel May went into business, opening a beauty parlor in her living room. The local women sought her out and she did surprisingly well, even to the point of eventually buying a larger house. But the beauty parlor always remained in the living room.

Ethel May sacrificed much for her family. Nicholson remembered that his "mother" worked so hard that "she couldn't stand up anymore."

Young Jack lived in what one might describe as an abnormal home. He was constantly surrounded by females; besides the fact that he was living with three women, there was also a steady parade of female customers tromping through the house. He later ruefully commented that he was "fortunate" to have turned out the way he had, "because my environment normally would have made me a fag."

Young Nicholson had always enjoyed giving people nicknames. Ethel May was known as "Mud," which was short for Mudder, which was yet another variation on Mother. His "sister" Lorraine, whom everyone else called Lor, was dubbed "Rain." Later, when Lorraine married her husband, George, Nicholson gave him the moniker "Shorty." About those early years of his life, Jack was later to say of George/Shorty that he was "as good a [substitute] father as anybody's ever going to get or need."

The one person in his life who apparently had no nickname was his beautiful, mysterious older "sister," June. There are some who have speculated that Nicholson always suspected, somewhere deep in his soul, that June was more than just his sister. Certainly his relationship with her was very close. But they weren't long under the same roof.

June left Neptune City for the bright lights of show business when her son was only four years old. She went to Miami to become an Earl Carroll dancer. Eventually she had some modest success on the vaudeville circuit working with comic Pinky Lee. June was hardly a star, yet she was making a living—all the while blazing a trail for her son to follow. Her success, minor as it was, opened the eyes of an impressionable little boy who looked up to his "big sister" as if she were a show business idol.

June's life could easily serve as the basis of a five-handkerchief movie. After leaving her son behind in the care of her mother to become a show girl, she eventually joined the war effort and worked in the control tower at a major military airport. Enter a famous test pilot, who also happened to be the son of a fabulously wealthy Long Island surgeon. The two fell in love, married, and had children of their own. Was little Jack forgotten? Happily, no. June invited him to stay with her and the family at their exclusive estate during the summers; it was a far cry from the gritty lower-middle-class life he led during the rest of the year in Neptune City. And June? She seemed more glamorous to her "little brother" than ever before. She was still beautiful, she wore exquisite clothing, and she moved among the rich and powerful.

Then midnight arrived—and the fairy tale ended not with a crash but with a slow, relentless descent into tragedy. June's marriage crumbled over a drinking problem. Not knowing where else to go, June went home to her mother. And to her son. For a while, she tried to put her life back together by teaching at Arthur Murray's dance studio in New York. When that didn't work out, she did what so many Americans at loose ends do, she headed for California. With her kids in tow—except Jack—she drove to the land of orange groves and got a job in an aircraft factory and later became a secretary. Bright, quick, wanting more out of life, June once again began the job of bettering herself, and soon became an assistant buyer for the J. C. Penney department store chain. Things were looking up. Until she was suddenly diagnosed with cancer.

By this time, Jack was a young man who had gone out to Hollywood to make his way in the movies. He hadn't gotten very far. June was his lifeline, his family away from home. They were as close as ever, and her illness hit him hard. She was in Cedars of Lebanon Hospital when Ethel May and Lorraine joined Nicholson at her bedside just before the end. Lorraine painfully recalled, ''We tried to talk about everything but what had brought us together that night. As we said our good-byes and headed toward the elevator, June called to her brother: 'Jack, shall I wait?' Jack blanched and tilted his head to one side. I knew what he was thinking. During the past six months, he had seen her shrink from one hundred twenty to eighty pounds and age fifty years. The pain was unrelenting, and her only wish—and ours—was that God would remove her from this agony. 'No,' Jack replied, looking away. When the door of the elevator closed, Jack slumped to the floor, sobbing hysterically. June died the following day at the age of forty-four.''

Even then, nobody told Nicholson the truth: that his mother had just died. It wasn't until roughly ten years later, when Nicholson was making *The Fortune* (1975) with Warren Beatty, that he received the shocking news. ''Someone called me on the phone—I think it was turned over by the investigative reporting for the *Time* cover story they did on me. Ultimately I got official verification from Lorraine. I was stunned.'' By then, however, Mud had also died. And with the passing of them both, any chance

Nicholson had of learning the name of his real father died with them.

As an actor, Nicholson must have appreciated the decades-long role-playing of Mud, Rain, and June. In all those years, they were never out of character, each one essaying their part to perfection. Nonetheless, the foundation of his childhood had to have been severely rocked. It was rough enough to have been the child of a drunkard father who had abandoned the family. But to later discover that those he loved most had perpetrated a massive deception upon him must have caused the ground to shift beneath his feet.

Yet Nicholson was able to look back at his life with a certain calm and cool reflection. ''June and I had so much in common,'' he would later tell an interviewer. ''We both fight hard. It didn't do her any good not to tell me, but she didn't because you never know how I would've reacted when I was younger.''

In the end, Nicholson fully understood why he wasn't told the truth. And he accepted it, perhaps even loving those who fooled him even more for their deception. ''Why would they tell me the truth?'' he asked rhetorically of Ovid Demaris, a writer who finally broke the story to the public a decade after Nicholson himself had learned the truth. ''Look,'' he explained, ''there are no Jackie Robinsons in this area. Illegitimacy is still the heaviest prejudice in the world . . . So that must be the reason, plus the fact that I'm incapable of keeping a secret. They probably just wanted to save me a lot of problems.'' Which, no doubt, they did.

Nicholson later emphatically explained, ''I'm very contra my constituency in terms of abortion because I'm positively against it. I don't have the right to any other view. My only emotion is gratitude, literally, for my life. [If June and Ethel had been] of less character, I would never have gotten to live. These women gave me the gift of life.''

Nonetheless, many of those who knew him in his youth, as well as many of those who befriended him later in life, have noted the same compelling feature in Nicholson's personality. As one childhood friend put it, "Jack's got a real hurt deep down inside, and there's no way of resolving it, ever."

CHAPTER 2

The Weaver

IF YOUNG JACK FOUND his inspiration for show business in June's short vaudeville success, he found his outlet as a performer in school. "I remember in fourth grade," he recalled, "I got sent to the corner next to the blackboard . . . and I powdered my face with chalk dust and made myself into a clown." (Or an early version of the Joker?) "That's the way I was all through high school," he continued. "The class clown, performing on and off the stage."

And he was glib. There wasn't another one among his crowd who could talk like young Jack. Ed Connor, an old friend from their days together at Roosevelt Elementary School, said, "I always chose Jack first when we played ball. Not so much for his hitting, but because Jack was good for at least two runs before we got up to bat. He could convince you of anything. He was the best con man I ever met." It was that ability to convince that enabled him to talk his school principal into taking his class on a field trip to see the movie *My Friend Flicka*. "When Jack saw a movie he liked," added Connor, "everyone had to see it. We once sat through *The Babe Ruth Story* five straight times."

This young boy who loved to give nicknames was soon given a string of his own. He went from "Jackie" to the far more hip "Nick" to "The Weaver," the last of these because of his ability to spin and weave wildly fantastic and intricate stories.

At first, he was mostly a cutup in class. By the time he

reached the eighth grade, though, young Nicholson finally began to channel his creative energies into more socially acceptable avenues, thanks, in part, to a kindly young teacher named Virginia Doyle. She recalled Nicholson's first flowering as a performer in a school show: "The year I remember most vividly was when Jack, dressed in a slit skirt and off-the-shoulder blouse, led a conga line of similarly dressed Carmen Miranda look-alike boys to the tune of 'Managua Nicaragua.' Jack, of course, was in front of the line, waving the maracas. As usual, he was the leader."

Nicholson had his troubles in the middle school years, caused, ironically enough, by the fact that he was too smart. He was considered so intelligent that he skipped seventh grade, making him a full year younger than his new classmates. It wrecked his early chances for a hot social life with the girls because they were all older than he was. Besides, as Mrs. Doyle pointed out, young Jack "was inclined to be chubby and quite short."

In later years he would more than make up for his inability to get girls as a youth. In the meantime, The Weaver not only entertained his friends with his intricately told stories, he also filled his own head with crazy fantasies . . . such as becoming an actor. Mrs. Doyle was often the recipient of young Jack's childhood thoughts, lending a sympathetic ear to his earnest dreams. "He never said he wanted to make it big on the silver screen," she recalled, "but he talked about acting all the time, and, of course, was always the first to volunteer for any variety show. But in the back of my mind I always thought he'd have a brilliant career in public relations or some business in which he could relate to people."

At the end of the eighth grade, both Jack and Mrs. Doyle let down their defenses and wept at their parting. She had grown close to the boy, and he had found a kindred spirit in her. Often, there is one teacher in a student's academic career who has a genuine impact, and Mrs. Doyle was clearly that teacher for the future Hollywood icon.

* * *

Nicholson went on to Manasquan High School, where he developed that uncanny ability to appeal to both the arty crowd and the jocks. To this day, and throughout his years as a star, he has been that rare actor whom the intelligentsia praise yet whom the average moviegoer also loves. The seeds of that ability to please all factions can be found back in New Jersey.

For instance, a high school classmate innocently touched on the dichotomy when he said, "The funny thing was, Jack hated school. He never studied, but he got the best grades. We always tried to copy off him during quizzes." In actuality, Nicholson always downplayed his achievements as a student because he didn't want to be perceived as an egghead.

Of course, the key to male acceptance in high school has been, and always will be, sports. Nicholson was the student manager of the high school basketball team when he was a sophomore. He even went so far as to destroy a competing team's equipment when he thought they had cheated his squad. He immediately admitted that he had done the deed, and was forced to get a job to pay for the damage. Yet one can imagine that his bold action in support of his team brought him the respect of many of his fellow students.

On the social level, he was everybody's buddy. "His smile was terrific," high school friend George Anderson told an interviewer. "He made plenty of friends who spanned several classes."

Another classmate, Alan Keith, fondly recalled, "He was always the first guy to do anything, it seemed."

Yet another friend concurred, remembering that "Jack was the first guy around to wear a ducktail haircut, pegged pants, blue suede shoes, and a one-button roll."

Nicholson himself later admitted that he had been "in competition with the school for entertainment value. I was even in high school plays, much to the horror of my immediate peers."

Yet he kept his friends in all camps.

When asked why he became involved in the theater during high school, Nicholson said, "I got sort of talked into it by a teacher. And all the chicks that I liked were doing plays—rehearsals after school with Sandra, that kind of thing." He also conceded, "I was a fat boy for a couple of years in high school, and that made me uptight for a while. You know, I couldn't get to enough girls." He has since more than made up for that lack, as the reader will soon learn.

In any event, by the time graduation rolled around, Nicholson had come to a personal crossroads. "I enjoyed school, but I wasn't into learning," he admitted. "I met the requirements in order to enjoy what I liked about school—being around a lot of people and having a good time."

The fact that he had a good time was clear enough—he had been voted Class Clown by his fellow students. His dual personality was also laid bare when he was voted both Class Optimist and Class Pessimist. His fellow students were way ahead of their time when they also voted him Best Actor. Finally, however, the evidence of his popularity wasn't in which titles he was given, but the fact that he was voted so many of them! He later recalled, "My [high school] contemporaries always had the ability to enjoy me."

But Nicholson hadn't fully enjoyed himself. Though he had college board scores that put him among the top two percent of the nation's high school seniors, he wasn't interested in continuing his schooling. "I could have had a Dupont chemical engineering scholarship [to the University of Delaware]," he said, "but I didn't really think that was my field. And I was kind of tired of school."

So, at the age of seventeen, he walked away from a chance for a free college education. The real reason behind his refusal to take the scholarship was that he felt he wasn't ready. He had skipped a grade and believed he was too young to go to college. His original plan was to take a year off before heading to the university. "Well," he later conceded, "by the time I had waited a year, I didn't want to go at all." He never regretted it, later saying that most of the people he knew who went to college told him that the years were wasted.

If he didn't go to college, though, what was he going to do with that year while he waited to grow older? He wasn't quite sure. It was Lorraine who convinced him to get out of Neptune City so he might see what the larger world offered.

The former "Best Actor" at Manasquan High School took her advice and left for Hollywood in 1954 . . .

CHAPTER 3

Life on the Fringe

HE WAS SEVENTEEN YEARS OLD, with no skills, no training, and only the vaguest notion of what it took to break into the movie business. He moved in with June and her two kids, and soon found work in a toy store, occasionally picking up a few extra bucks as a pool hall hustler.

It was not a glittering tinsel-town existence.

After several miserable months had passed, Nicholson became totally discouraged. He called Lorraine to tell her she could expect him home real soon. He was giving up.

That was as close as Hollywood would get to losing one of its future stars. Before he could leave, however, a job in the MGM cartoon department surfaced, and Nicholson grabbed it. His work seemed like a surreal joke: sorting fan mail for the animated cat-and-mouse team of Tom and Jerry. He was paid thirty dollars per week, but at least he had a toehold in the movie business.

Legends surround the beginnings of many a matinee idol. Nicholson is no different. The story goes that as a cocky young employee at MGM, he made it his business to greet all the big studio executives by their first names, as if he were their equal. When he pulled that stunt on Joe Pasternak, the producer of such MGM hits as *Summer Stock* (1950) and *The Great Caruso* (1951), the older man peered at Nicholson, studied him for a moment, and then offered him a screen test.

It might have all begun for Nicholson right there and then—just like that—except for one small detail: He didn't know what the hell he was doing. When given a script, the would-be actor didn't even know he was supposed to memorize his lines. He blew his first big break, turning his screen test into an embarrassing fiasco.

Pasternak, however, would not be thwarted. He used his influence to get his young find into the Player's Ring, a small Los Angeles theater group. And then he promptly forgot about him.

In reality, getting into the Player's Ring was the genuine break Nicholson needed. He had to learn his craft. Eventually he made his stage debut in a production of *Tea and Sympathy* with Michael Landon, Edd Byrnes, and Robert Fuller. While the others went on to success in TV (in, respectively, "Bonanza," "77 Sunset Strip," and "Wagon Train"), Nicholson remained thoroughly overlooked—a circumstance that deeply rankled.

His training, however, had only just begun. Over the ensuing years, Nicholson studied acting with Jeff Corey, Joe Flynn, Martin Landau, and Robert Vaughn. It was during this time that he met many of the young, creative people with whom he would work during the rest of his career. Among his fellow students were future producer/ director Roger Corman, actress Sally Kellerman, actor Dean Stockwell, and future screenwriters Carol Eastman and Robert Towne. His loose coterie of friends would expand and evolve over the next several decades, and Nicholson would do some of his most interesting and provocative work with these people.

In the beginning, though, it seemed as if he did more partying than acting. He developed quite a reputation as a carouser during the late 1950s and early 1960s. It wasn't that he was a big drinker; no way did he want to walk in the footsteps of the man he thought was his father. But he was known to drink some wine in his day. He was also known to be especially attractive to the ladies.

Nicholson reminisced about the old days in his Fountain Avenue house, where he threw many a wild party: "Harry Dean Stanton, who was one of my close sidekicks in those days, says that whenever he thinks of me in that period, he always sees me with a cheap red wine on my red lips. We'd get nineteen half-gallons of Gallo Mountain Red and get everybody drunk. I guess you could call them orgies by the strictest definition . . . There were a lot of rooms in my house, and people would take their own little private trips. I don't know what they were doing. I know what I was doing, though, and I guess that could be called an orgy. But it wasn't something where everybody's there and naked and fucking one another all over the place. I've never been in that scene. I've tried ineffectively to promote it a time or two, because of thrill-seeking impulses, but they never really came together. I've never been in an orgy of more than three people.''

Jack Nicholson was deadly with the ladies long before he became a household name. Short, slightly built, not conventionally handsome at all, a struggling actor who was perpetually broke, he hardly seemed the type to bed so many beautiful young would-be actresses. But he was hell on wheels. Or, rather, hell on a mattress. The killer smile, for which he has since become famous, was already a lethal weapon in those years.

There were hot and cold running women in his Fountain Avenue house, most of them hot, very few of them cold, and all of them running to Nicholson. Yet Nicholson wasn't a "wolf." Besides his smile, intelligence, and charm, his greatest asset was that he was a terrific listener. For instance, actress Sally Kellerman recalled, "I would sit on Jack's lap and pour out my heart to him."

Many a woman started on his lap and ended in his bed, the vast majority of them actresses whose most memorable Hollywood credits now include a night with Jack Nicholson.

Sex wasn't the only item on the menu. Drugs were being served as well. Specifically marijuana. In the beginning, he was discreet about it, smoking behind closed doors or in secluded places. Later, after his success in *Easy Rider,* he became refreshingly outspoken, if foolish, stating in *People* magazine, ''I love to get high. I'd say, about four days a week. I think that's about average for an American.''

He got flak for that, but it's part of Nicholson's unique cheek that he can get away with outlandish comments and actions without suffering career-crippling reactions. His audience—men and women alike—see him as a reflection of themselves and admire the fact that he will smile and boast, ''I've balled everybody, taken all the drugs, gone everywhere.''

Both before and after his early Hollywood years full of dope and sexual escapades, there was a stretch of time—nearly half a dozen years—in which he was also an old-fashioned married man.

Sandra Knight was a strikingly beautiful, dark-haired actress who was part of the B-movie circuit. Nicholson met her in Jeff Corey's acting class, where they discovered that they had more in common than their ambition. Sandra had been living with actor Robert (''Baretta'') Blake at the time, but when that ended, she and the refugee from Neptune City formed a close bond, getting married in 1962. It was B-movie heaven, at least for a little while. The two starred in Roger Corman's *The Terror* (1963), which was the only time they appeared together on film. In that same year, they had a daughter, Jennifer, with whom Nicholson has maintained a protective and loving relationship throughout the years. After Jennifer was born, Sandra retired from the movie business to devote herself to her child and her husband.

No marriage ends for a single reason, and there were several pressures that doomed their relationship. One reason was Nicholson's driving desire to succeed in Hollywood; he became a workaholic, acting by day and writing by night. ''I simply didn't have time to ask for peace and quiet or to say, 'Well, now, wait a second, maybe you're being unreasonable,' '' he reflected in a conversation with an interviewer. ''I didn't have the thirty minutes I felt the conversation needed,'' he continued. ''If the other person can't see that I haven't got time right now, I can't explain it to her. I've blown a lot of significant relationships in my life because I was working and didn't have the time to deal with a major crisis.'' In the description of his frustration, one can sense the eerie similarity between his real life and that scene in *The Shining* (1980) when, as writer Jack Torrance, he blows up in a frustrated rage when his wife (Shelley Duvall) interrupts him at the typewriter.

Another reason for the breakup was that ''the secret inner pressure about monogamy'' was becoming too much for him to bear. Unable to remain faithful, he ended the relationship and would soon become involved with some of the most beautiful and fascinating women in Hollywood (more on that later).

Yet another contributing factor to the split was Nicholson's medically supervised experimentation with LSD in the mid-1960s. The relationship with Sandra was already on the rocks by this time, but his wife's own previously bad experience with acid (as LSD was more commonly known) was enough to drive the two of them even further apart.

Unlike many divorces, Nicholson's was happily lacking in recriminations. ''My divorce was good, like the marriage was. It was a clear, nonviolent, nontumultuous decision. My wife, Sandra, and I had just come to a very real separating of the ways. It was obviously the only thing to do, and we did it very simply. The probable cause,'' he explained in this instance, ''was that she became stimulated in a mystical area, and I couldn't get with that. I didn't want to get caught in a situation where I was in competition with God, or something like that.''

Competing with other actors for decent roles was competition enough. And Nicholson had much to learn on that score.

Describing his impressions of the neophyte thespian during those early years, acting teacher Jeff Corey said, ''He worked hard, but at times I grew impatient with him. There was sometimes a physically leaden quality in his voice, which he now knows how to use very well. I remember once taking a walk around the block with him and telling him to get a little élan into his work." Corey also remembered that Nicholson was "a ballsy, fun-loving kid, not shy in the least, intelligent, with a kind of nice, old-fashioned good looks, and easy to deal with. Never got pissed off or uptight about criticism." Well, at least not too often. Once, however, Corey gave Nicholson a hard time, telling him there was no "poetry" in his work. "Maybe, Jeff," Nicholson shot back, "you don't see the poetry I'm showing you."

Nicholson pounded the pavement in search of acting jobs, except there didn't seem to be any in the offing. He didn't have the conventional good looks of the traditional Hollywood leading man. For that matter, he was hardly a man; he was still just a teenager.

In the course of his auditioning, though, there was one casting agent who must have been psychic. He told Nicholson, "I don't know what we'd ever use you for, but if we need you, we'll need you very badly." Truer words were never spoken. It would take nearly fifteen years, though, before the major studios would begin clamoring for his services.

Meanwhile, Nicholson scraped by with some television work, appearing in such shows as "Matinee Theater" and "Divorce Court." Of the latter, the actor would later joke that "I was the most unabashed corespondent in town."

That offbeat quality in Nicholson that the casting agent had noticed was antithetical to the white bread quality of television in those years. So the struggling actor had a brainstorm. In order to get attention, to separate himself from the crowd, this unemployed actor turned a negative into a positive by making the outlandish announcement, "Nicholson doesn't do television!"

"I swear to you," writer/producer Don Devlin said, "that as a result of this, people began talking about how Jack Nicholson would not do television. The word went out. And it wasn't long after that that Jack started working for Corman . . .''

Roger Corman. He became famous as the King of the B's, making a remarkable string of low-budget movies that began during the mid-1950s. A producer, director, and mentor, he made movies in virtually every genre, from science fiction to horror, and from biker movies to drug films. He usually shot on shoestring budgets, with ridiculously short production schedules, threadbare sets, equally nonexistent scripts, and either totally unknown actors or has-beens. But he made his movies with flair and imagination. Just as important, he also knew his audience: the disaffected, alienated postwar, postbomb youth.

Corman probably helped more people get their start in Hollywood than any other single individual. Among directors, he gave Francis Ford Coppola, Martin Scorsese, Jonathan Demme, and Peter Bogdanovich their early opportunities to make movies. Among actors, his great claim to fame is his discovery of Jack Nicholson.

The two had met in Jeff Corey's class, which Corman had taken in order to gain insight into directing actors. Sometime later, when Corman was casting for his 1958 film *Cry Baby Killer,* he decided to give Nicholson the lead. It was the actor's very first motion picture, and he was handed the starring role!

''I picked Jack for the lead because I thought he had then what he has today,'' Corman said. ''I thought he was an intelligent and exciting actor,'' he continued, ''a very inventive and creative actor who could bring more to a role than what was written in the script. I thought he had a youthful energy and at the same time a certain amount of control over that energy.''

In *Cry Baby Killer,* Nicholson played a misunderstood, James Dean–like character who believes that he killed two guys who had attacked his girlfriend. Loaded with teenage angst, the movie was made in ten days on a budget of a measly seven thousand dollars.

Like most el cheapo movies, it was ignored by the majority of critics, particularly in the United States. Ironically, though, it was appreciated in England by the prestigious publication *Films and Filming*.

"Jack was very good in it," said Corman.

"I thought, within a few weeks, I'd be a star," Nicholson ruefully recalled. "I didn't get another acting job for nine months."

CHAPTER 4

The Killer B's

MORE OFTEN THAN NOT, whenever Nicholson appeared in movies during the 1960s, he could be found in a Roger Corman production. The actor has often publicly expressed his gratitude, saying that "Roger really carried me for about seven years. He was the only guy that I ever got a job from." The latter statement is only a modest exaggeration. Nicholson acted in, wrote, and/or produced twenty films before he became a mainstream star in *Easy Rider* (1969), and more than half of those films were made by Corman.

Nicholson shot up and down cast lists during the years he wandered the B-movie wilderness. And not only did he have a surprising mix of both lead roles and minor appearances in his films, he also played an astonishing range of characters, from romantic heroes to vicious killers, and from best friends to comic relief roles. And just as his mentor Corman made films in all genres, so did Nicholson appear in movies from most of the major categories, including period pieces, comedies, horror films, westerns, gangster movies, contemporary dramas, thrillers, etcetera.

The films were not always good; in fact, they often were bad. And the same could be said of Nicholson; he later admitted as much, saying, "The first movies I made are so unbearable to me because all I can see is this young kid who's trying to sort of dive sideways onto the screen, sort of hurl himself into a movie career, and that's all I see, is this kind of fearful, tremulous, naked, desperate ambition. Which is pathetic.''

Nonetheless, Corman taught him the same lesson that Napoleon had once learned: '' *'Vite, vite, plus vite.'* Which,'' according to Nicholson, ''means 'fast, fast, faster.' Roger was a no-bull school. You had to get in the swing or get out.''

Nicholson got in the swing.

One of his earliest, yet most arresting performances was a minor but memorable role in Corman's *Little Shop of Horrors* (1960). Shot in a miraculous two days, this black comedy has become a latter-day classic, inspiring a hit musical play and a big-budget movie musical produced by Steven Spielberg. In the original film, about a plant that needs human blood to survive, Nicholson's famous scene was shot in a mere two hours. He played the role of a masochistic patient named Wilbur Force, who, with unconcealed glee, visits a sadistic dentist, insisting, ''No novocaine—it dulls the senses!'' It was a fabulous comic turn, one of the rare instances during his nonstar years when he had the opportunity to show his comic ability. Later, Bill Murray would play the same part in the musical version of the film made in 1986.

In the same year that he made *Little Shop of Horrors,* Nicholson had a shot at mainstream Hollywood success when he won an important supporting role in the adaptation of the classic James T. Farrell work *Studs Lonigan.* Nicholson claimed he got the part because he, alone, volunteered to read all three volumes of the *Studs Lonigan* trilogy. He might have saved himself the effort. The film failed miserably at the box office and quickly sank out of sight. And with it, Nicholson sank as well, disappearing back into the murky B-movie underground.

He bobbed up to the surface in a mainstream film only one more time during the 1960s, playing a sailor in *Ensign*

Pulver (1964). He was last in the cast list, which included, among others, Robert Walker, Jr. (in the title role), Burl Ives, Walter Matthau, Tommy Sands, Millie Perkins, Kay Medford, Larry Hagman, James Farentino, and James Coco. Produced and directed by the esteemed Joshua Logan, the big-budget movie from Warner Bros. was a critical and commercial disaster.

As Nicholson often said, he didn't work in the exploitation market because he liked it, but because it was the only work he could get.

In his B-movie roles, Nicholson shuttled back and forth between playing good guys and bad guys. In such films as *Too Soon to Love* (1960), an early low-budget teen movie about abortion, Nicholson played the supporting role of the hero's best friend. In *The Wild Ride* (1960), he had top billing as a psychopath who wreaks havoc in a small town à la Marlon Brando in *The Wild One* (1954). He also played a wronged youth in a dreadful western called *The Broken Land* (1962), and a soulful hero named Poet in *Hell's Angels on Wheels* (1967), before turning the psychological tables and giving life to the outrageously evil character of Bunny in yet another biker opus, *Rebel Rousers* (1967). One could sense the danger in his persona in the latter film. While the actor's ''killer smile'' would later refer to his way with the ladies, in many of his early movies, it was used more literally for its menace.

One of Nicholson's most well-known films during this era is also among Roger Corman's more memorable movies. The producer/director, who had already begun making a name for himself in a cycle of stylishly campy Edgar Allan Poe adaptations starring Vincent Price, gave Nicholson a major role in *The Raven*, a horror-comedy that starred Price and featured the famous, but fading, Hollywood stars Peter Lorre and Boris Karloff. Nicholson played Peter Lorre's son—in retrospect, an inspired bit of casting—and (despite sixth billing) was the film's ostensible romantic hero. Both the film and Nicholson were lightly likable and well received by both the audience and the critics.

The Terror, another Corman horror movie, literally followed on the heels of *The Raven.* It seemed to be an ill-conceived (one might say unconceived) film that came into existence for no better reason than that Corman wrapped *The Raven* two days early, and the sets and costumes—already paid for—were still available for another forty-eight hours. Corman thrived on opportunities like this, and he immediately decided to make another movie, despite the glaring lack of a script, let alone a plot.

Made in something more than two days (though not much more), *The Terror* looked like a far more expensive film—thanks to the sets and costumes—than it actually was. The story was a concoction created as the cameras rolled, and which was later embellished during the editing process. In the film, Nicholson plays a lost soldier during the Napoleonic era who sets off after a beautiful girl (then wife Sandra Knight) who saved his life and then vanished. He finds her in the castle of Baron Von Lepp (Boris Karloff), only to discover that he has fallen in love with an apparition of a long dead woman who, when freed of Von Lepp's spell, turns to dust in Nicholson's arms at picture's end.

Moody and romantic, but also silly and disjointed, *The Terror* has its moments. That it works at all is a tribute to those who helped Corman make it. Though uncredited, both Francis Ford Coppola and Monte Hellman directed portions of the film, as did Nicholson. In addition, Nicholson helped write the script. All told, it was an experience that only whetted Nicholson's appetite for more work behind the camera.

And no wonder. Despite the fact that, as one friend put it, "He always thought of himself as a movie star," the sad truth was that Nicholson seemed buried in B-movie quicksand. The actor later would say, "I looked familiar. Only problem: Nobody recognized me." He was beginning to worry that he'd never make it to the big time. If that was the case, then perhaps it was time to use his talents as "The Weaver" again and consider *making* movies instead of starring in them.

CHAPTER 5

Jack of All Trades

IN 1963, NICHOLSON WAS twenty-six years old and watching many of the people he knew during the latter half of the 1950s going on to fame and fortune while he still struggled along from picture to picture.

A pragmatist underneath his bohemian life-style, Nicholson decided it was time to make some changes. He hadn't gone out to Hollywood to necessarily be an actor; he could also be a writer, or a producer, or even a director. Why not? In the fluid world of the low-budget, independent movie, creative people were constantly shuttling between one sort of job and another, picking up experience, knowledge, and (if they were lucky) a good credit on a sleeper hit that might catapult them to a job with a major studio.

Corman himself suggested that Nicholson try his hand at screenwriting. The producer/director had been impressed with Jack's nimble storytelling ability during the rush to create a plot out of thin air for *The Terror*. Nicholson, however, might have also perceived a subtle hint in Corman's suggestion (i.e., that he had better find another way to make it in Hollywood besides being an actor).

So, with Corman's encouragement, and with nothing to lose, he teamed up with an old friend, Don Devlin, and wrote a screenplay in three weeks that was sold with surprising ease to Associated Producers, Inc., the B-movie arm of 20th Century-Fox. The resulting film, *Thunder Island* (1963), won plaudits from no less an industry bible than *Variety*, which said, "A commendable example of frankly B picture craftsmanship . . . pound for pound, dollar for dollar, a cut above average . . . The scenario is a workmanlike original.''

Though he didn't appear in *Thunder Island*, Nicholson hadn't given up on acting. Clever and resourceful, he came upon the ideal method of pursuing both his writing and his performing by penning scripts for himself. He found a talented and willing accomplice in director Monte Hellman. Kindred spirits who respected each other's talents, they became partners and soon began their own series of provocative collaborations, making four pictures together during the mid-1960s.

Their first two film projects were a couple of action quickies made in the Philippines, *Back Door to Hell* (1964) and *Flight to Fury* (1966). Having already written a reasonably well reviewed and financially successful movie, Nicholson was given the opportunity to write the second of these two films while playing lead roles in both.

Despite the presence of popular teen singing star Jimmie Rodgers (who remains far more famous for his song ''Kisses Sweeter than Wine'' than he does for his acting career), *Back Door to Hell* set no fires at the box office. Far more interesting was *Flight to Fury,* which was based on a story concocted by Hellman and the film's producer, Fred Roos, and then scripted by Nicholson. On the surface, Nicholson's script about a quest for stolen diamonds offers no surprises—except in regard to his own character, the villain, Jay Wickam. Once again essaying a crazed baddie, he brought to the role (in both his writing of it and in his playing) a richness rarely found in bargain-basement B's. Nicholson recalls the film as ''the one where I kill myself,'' but he has also said, ''That's one of my early movies I do like.''

After Nicholson and Hellman returned from the Philippines, Roger Corman gave them the backing to make two westerns. The films that emerged, *The Shooting* (1966), written by Carol Eastman as Adrien Joyce, and *Ride in the Whirlwind* (1966), became the high point of Nicholson's work as an independent filmmaker. Both movies were produced by Nicholson and Hellman, giving them an unusual degree of control over their projects. Coupled with the fact that Nicholson also starred in both and wrote *Ride in the Whirlwind,* there was every reason to expect that these two westerns would be considerably different from run-of-the-mill B movies.

And they are.

They were made for a mere seventy-five thousand dollars per film, and Nicholson later told an interviewer, "Not a single other human being could have made those films at that price, costumed at Western Costume, thirty-five-millimeter, color . . . I did it by doing everything myself. Monte Hellman, my former partner, cut it; I assisted. Monte directed; we coproduced . . . We had short crews, worked long hours. People did favors. But you can't expect them to do favors forever." In other words, these films had to make money or there would be no more favors forthcoming.

Turning these two films into hits, however, was a daunting task, because they were anything but commercial projects. *The Shooting* nearly defies plot description; it is a psychological and philosophical western that owes more to Albert Camus than it does to John Ford. Nicholson, playing a laconic killer, starred, along with Warren Oates, Will Hutchins, and Millie Perkins.

Ride in the Whirlwind is a bleak and elusive movie, rich with layered meanings. In contrast to his role in *The Shooting,* Nicholson plays an innocent man forced to go on the run to save his life. The other leads were Cameron Mitchell and Millie Perkins.

Both films are ambiguous to an extreme. Nicholson called them "existential westerns." As a consequence, they were initially considered totally uncommercial for the American market and were not released in the States. "It took a full year to do the two pictures," said Hellman. "And it took another year to sell them. Jack spent a long time taking them around to festivals in Europe."

Nicholson's efforts paid off as he almost single-handedly

turned the films into hits on the Continent, especially France, where they were not only popular with the public, but with the critics, as well. Speaking about his early B movies, Nicholson would later say, ''They were usually exploitation pictures, but you were sometimes able to sneak some quality into them. Actually, I'm very proud of some of them.'' No doubt he had these two films in mind.

Ironically, it wasn't until 1972, when Nicholson was a bona fide mainstream star, that *The Shooting* and *Ride in the Whirlwind* were released theatrically in the United States. And even then, they were too exotic and strange for the American paying public.

While he was peddling his two westerns, Corman offered Nicholson one of the more significant supporting roles in the producer/director's first major studio film, the gangster opus *The St. Valentine's Day Massacre* (1967). The movie starred Jason Robards and George Segal, and Nicholson only had to say yes to have the role of a Capone gang member. Corman had designed the film to be largely built around the murders of each of Capone's cronies, and Nicholson would have had a chance to shine in a featured role. He turned it down flat. The reason? Nicholson needed money, so he opted for the role of a driver who only had a couple of lines but who, because of the film's shooting schedule, had to be available for a longer period of time and therefore earned more money. As a result, in a minuscule role in *The St. Valentine's Day Massacre*, Nicholson had his biggest payday as an actor in ten years, far surpassing his *star* salary on any one of Corman's low-budget quickies.

It was a sad commentary, though, that after nearly a decade in the movie business, he felt compelled to take a lesser role in order to make more money. As an actor, it seemed he was destined to remain on Hollywood's fringe. Perhaps even on the fringe of Hollywood's fringe. As he later lamented, ''I couldn't even get interviewed for *The Graduate* (1967). They saw every actor I had lunch with.''

He was clearly becoming dispirited. ''When I was paying my dues in this business," he said, "I constantly maintained that I was as good as anybody around. But unless somebody else says that about you, there's no way to believe it totally."

Nicholson was thirty; he'd been in Hollywood for thirteen years. If he didn't make something big happen soon, there was every reason to believe that it might not happen at all.

CHAPTER 6

On the Trip

TIMES WERE CHANGING. The underground youth culture—the hippie movement—with its drugs and antiestablishment attitude, was about to make its cinematic assault on the mainstream. Nicholson was into the drug scene, and he certainly wasn't part of the (Hollywood) establishment. That combination of factors, coupled with talent and timing, led to a series of events that catapulted him to stardom.

He had smoked marijuana for quite some time, but beginning in the mid-1960s, he also took an interest in the new mind expansion drug LSD. His experience with acid may or may not have expanded his mind, but it certainly expanded his career.

"The first time I took acid myself was part of an experiment by a psychiatrist at UCLA," Nicholson said. "It changed my life . . . The psychiatrist blindfolded me for the first five hours. I regressed, re-experienced my own birth, was in the womb. It's hard to verbalize this kind of thing. I was an infant thinking I was wetting myself and talking with a small voice. I even felt like I was going to die. The doctor said, 'Let yourself go.' I did. I died. It was liberating. Then my wife came to get me. I mixed her up with my mother. And all the while I'm schizo and could look at myself. And I was going with it. The old actor training. Go with it. I used the experience in writing *The Trip.*"

He used more than his drug-related experience when he wrote the screenplay for this Roger Corman film starring

33

Peter Fonda, Susan Strasberg, Bruce Dern, and Dennis Hopper. Nicholson essentially patterned the entire script on his own life. He later conceded, ''Most of my divorce is written into *The Trip.*''

Take a look at the similarities. Just like Nicholson, Fonda played a man who worked in the media and whose marriage was in deep trouble. Desperate to find the meaning of his life, Fonda takes a hit of LSD. The events Fonda experiences under the influence of the drug are much the same as those that Nicholson described: witnessing his own death, and so forth. And the end result of the trip is also the same—the dissolution of his marriage—but now that he is ''reborn'' with a new vision of himself, he also has the chance to create a new life.

Whether the screenplay was autobiographical or not meant nothing to American International Pictures, the famous youth exploitation movie company that was backing the picture. They saw dollar signs. It was a movie that they accurately guessed stood right on the crest of a new tidal wave of drug-related movies.

No such film had yet to be produced in Hollywood, and the field was wide open to AIP. Certainly no major studio in 1967 would touch a movie extolling the virtues of LSD. But the audience was ripe. Acid was not against the law at that time, and it was getting a great deal of attention in the media, especially in the recording business. For instance, the Beatles had a hit at about that time with ''Lucy in the Sky with Diamonds,'' which, despite the Fab Four's protestations, most everyone thought stood for LSD; certainly the lyrics suggested the sights and sounds of an acid trip.

Unfortunately, neither AIP nor the company's principal producer/director, Roger Corman, saw Nicholson as an actor in the film, even though he had actually written himself a part in the movie, that of Fonda's best friend, who sees him through his trip. Bruce Dern got the part.

It had to have been a humbling disappointment to be turned down for a role he had written for himself. And there wasn't anything he could do about it. Corman had kept Nicholson alive throughout most of the 1960s with acting jobs as well as several writing and producing opportunities, so he could hardly turn on his mentor and hold the screenplay hostage in return for the part (as Sylvester Stallone did with *Rocky*).

If it hurt to lose the role, there were compensations. Big ones. The most immediate was the huge commercial success of *The Trip*. The movie was such a "happening" that it was also heavily reviewed. The critics gave it mixed notices, although even bad reviews were better than the usual—being totally ignored. Besides, the audience for this film didn't care what the old, established critics had to say; this was *their* film.

Having opened the cinema door to "psychedelic" movies, Nicholson was rewarded with a lead role in AIP's *Psych-Out* (1968), joining a cast that included Susan Strasberg, Dean Stockwell, Bruce Dern, Adam Rourke, and Henry Jaglom. *Psych-Out*, like *The Trip*, was full of special effects, splashes of weird colors, odd angles, and bizarre events that were intended to suggest a world seen through a pharmaceutical haze. The movie made its money and then quietly disappeared.

Meanwhile, Nicholson was back in the producing game, joining director Bob Rafelson and film company executive Bert Schneider for the first of a string of collaborations, an intriguing flop called *Head* (1968). Nicholson was heavily involved behind the camera, cowriting and coproducing the movie with Rafelson, with Schneider acting as executive producer.

Head is a slang term that, in the late 1960s and early 1970s, had come to describe anyone who smoked a lot of dope, as in a "pothead." The film, as you might therefore imagine, was yet another entry in the drug-related wave of films that hit the marketplace after *The Trip*. But the movie was scorned by the critics and ignored by the public. It has, however, developed something of a cult following over the years. It's no wonder that it intrigues people today. The cast list includes not only the Monkees (three of whom have lately resurrected their act), but also Victor Mature, Annette Funicello, Carol Doda, Frank Zappa, and other strange surprises. Even Nicholson and Rafelson appear in the film as themselves for a brief instant.

Nicholson has referred to the movie as "anti–rock and roll." Perhaps that is one of the (many) reasons the film failed to find the young audience it needed upon its initial release. Nonetheless, the movie had one gigantic fan: Nicholson. "I saw it 158 million times," he gleefully told an interviewer. "I loved it!"

He must have thought that whatever minor clout he had in the business had been dissipated by the failure of *Head*. But it isn't necessarily what you've done, it's who you know. And thanks to working with Peter Fonda and Dennis Hopper on *The Trip,* and Bob Rafelson and Bert Schneider on *Head*, Nicholson had hooked up with the right people at the right time. He didn't know it, he didn't plan it, but the fact that he knew them would make all the difference in the world when a low-budget film titled *Easy Rider* came to be made the following year.

CHAPTER 7

Easy Rider

EASY RIDER OPENED on July 14, 1969, and quickly became a gigantic hit, earning more than $35 million and establishing itself as an instant classic. At a time when huge amounts of money had been spent and lost on colossal flops such as *Dr. Doolittle* (1967) and *Star!* (1968), the startling critical and financial success of this low-budget biker movie stunned the film industry. There were several effects. It unleashed a lot of money for small-budget films to independent filmmakers, most of whom failed. Also, Hollywood turned ersatz radical in the hope of capitalizing on the sudden popularity of the counterculture—and that also failed. More significantly, though, the major studios learned a lesson from *Easy Rider*: that the movie audience was no longer a family audience. Since that watershed film, a huge percentage of the movies of the 1970s and 1980s have been largely geared toward the young.

A more immediate result of *Easy Rider*'s success was the emergence of Nicholson as a potential new star. If the film was controversial—and it was—there was no controversy about him; Nicholson was unanimously praised for his twenty minutes or so of screen time by critics from every sort of publication you could imagine, from the respectable *New York Times* ("Nicholson is so good . . . that *Easy Rider* never quite recovers from his loss") to the avant-garde *The Village Voice* ("First and foremost is the sterling performance of Jack Nicholson").

The movie starred Peter Fonda (who also produced),

and Dennis Hopper (who also directed). Hopper was inspired to develop the story when he came across a magazine piece about two counterculture bikers who were murdered, their bodies found on the side of a lonely road. Initially written by the two stars, Nicholson later noted that "Terry Southern [the author of the best-seller *Candy*] was brought in as one of the writers so people wouldn't think it was just another Peter Fonda motorcycle flick." Eventually even Nicholson got in on the act, penning parts of the screenplay concerning Fonda's character.

There are ironies within ironies concerning Nicholson's involvement with *Easy Rider*. On the one hand, the film might never have been made without his behind-the-scenes help in putting the deal together. On the other hand, he was the *third* choice to play the naive lawyer George Hanson, and even then he was literally forced upon Hopper, who didn't want him for the role. Of course, Nicholson stole the show because his character gave the movie its heart. Audience members who weren't long-haired, drug-dealing, marijuana-smoking bikers could identify with Hanson. He was that pivotal transitional character, the person who crossed the line from "straight" society to find liberation in some of the attitudes and thoughts of the "hippie" element represented by Fonda and Hopper.

How does a classic get made? How is a star really born? In the case of *Easy Rider* and Nicholson, the two are closely bound together.

After Fonda and Hopper made *The Trip,* based on Nicholson's screenplay, they all got together and considered making a movie called *The Queen*. The script was a thinly veiled story about President Kennedy's assassination, with Nicholson as Robert McNamara, Fonda as McGeorge Bundy, Hopper as Dean Rusk, and Rip Torn as Lyndon Johnson. Nobody, however, was willing to put up money for such a project, and the movie was never made.

Fonda must have realized that the only way to make a serious film was to set it in a milieu in which he was already famous. Nicholson said, "Peter at that time had become the John Wayne of the bike movies.'' It made sense, therefore, to use the biker film format for his own ends.

"He [Fonda] came to me," said Roger Corman, explaining the genesis of *Easy Rider,* "and said he wanted to do it, that he would produce, I would be executive producer, Dennis would direct, and the deal would be with American International Pictures. I talked to Sam Arkoff [the head of AIP] and everything was set. We put the package together and started the preproduction planning." Not long after, however, Arkoff got worried; Hopper's reputation for dependability during those years was anything but solid. He insisted that if Hopper fell even one day behind schedule during the shoot, Arkoff would have the right to replace him as director. That effectively killed the deal.

Fonda and Hopper had to start all over. They needed funding and guaranteed distribution to make their picture, and so they began asking everyone they knew for help.

"They came in while I was writing and coproducing *Head,*" Nicholson recalled. "They came in with a bunch of pages, and I read it and knew it couldn't possibly lose any money. The twelve pages looked terrific." As far as Nicholson was concerned, "I knew that any motorcycle picture with Dennis Hopper and Peter Fonda in it was going to make a certain number of millions of dollars, because I was acquainted with the grossing potential of all those films." Nicholson himself had starred in a couple of them, and he knew from firsthand experience how much money they could make.

"At this point," Corman said, picking up the story, "Jack, who was now working with Bert Schneider and Rob Rafelson, suggested that Peter and Dennis bring the project over to them and they could make it at Columbia [the releasing studio for their company, BBS]. I remember very vividly that I lost a couple of million dollars by not being involved," Corman wryly concluded.

On Nicholson's recommendation, Schneider handed

Fonda and Hopper a check for $675,000. *Easy Rider* was back in business. Nicholson, though, was simply the conduit for the deal. He had brought the parties together but had nothing to show for it himself. And that's the way it would have stayed had there not been trouble during preproduction. Lots of trouble.

Early on, the only bona fide acting talent in the film, Rip Torn, had quit. Torn had been cast as George Hanson, and his loss was a blow. Apparently he and Hopper had gotten into an argument, and as one person who witnessed the fracas at a Beverly Hills party reported, Torn said, "I'm not going to do your shitty film."

With the role of George Hanson suddenly and unexpectedly available, one might have thought that the grateful Fonda and Hopper would have immediately thought of Nicholson. Not so. They went after Bruce Dern for the part, who turned them down. Dern was trying to get into the Hollywood mainstream and didn't want to get stuck in yet another low-budget motorcycle movie.

By the time the cast and crew were on location in New Orleans, the entire production had fallen into disarray. It looked as if the movie might never get made. A troubleshooter was needed, and Bert Schneider nominated Nicholson. He sent Jack down to New Orleans to straighten things out. "[It] all worked out great," said Nicholson. ". . . I got them Leslie Kovacs [the cinematographer]. I got them my production manager, who put a new crew together. By this time, Bert was a little uneasy, so he asked me to take this role [of George Hanson], largely because of the fact that I knew production, knew this crew, knew this situation."

In other words, Schneider wanted his own man watching over the production, looking after his investment. Whether Hopper understood Schneider's motives or not isn't known. What is known is that Hopper resisted; he didn't want Nicholson for the part. "I wanted to use a real Texan . . . It was my first picture, and I was really hung up on the idea of getting someone who had the accent," said Hopper. "I had never seen Jack do anything like that before. I saw him as a Hollywood flasher, not as a country bumpkin."

Finally, Schneider won the day and Hopper relented. Nicholson had the role of George Hanson. He also had practically no time to prepare himself for the part. In order to play the clean-cut lawyer who had become an alcoholic, Nicholson shaved off his beard, cut his hair, and searched for a pair of glasses that were identical to those worn by the alcoholic who (at that time) Nicholson thought was his father. As a prop, the glasses served to remind the method actor that a drunk could be sweet and gentle, meaning no harm to anyone. The glasses gave him a sense of character from the outside in. As for the Texas twang that Hopper was after, Nicholson borrowed his speech pattern from then President Lyndon Baines Johnson.

If Hopper harbored any lingering hostility over having Nicholson forced upon him, it was probably erased when the two took an acid trip together one night in Taos, New Mexico, at the tomb of their mutual literary hero, D. H. Lawrence. It was reportedly a mellow experience, but in the morning, Nicholson woke up in a tree without any recollection of how he got there.

Speaking of drugs, there was plenty of grass being smoked during the filming of the movie, some of it written into the script. For instance, Nicholson recalled that during his memorable campfire monologue, "Each time I did a take or an angle, it involved smoking almost an entire joint. We were smoking regular dope, pretty good Mexican grass from the state of Michoacán. Now, the main portion of this sequence is the transition from not being stoned to being stoned. So that after the first take or two, the acting job becomes reversed. Instead of being straight and having to act stoned at the end, I'm now stoned at the beginning and have to act straight and then gradually let myself return to where I was—which was very stoned. It was an unusual reverse acting problem. And Dennis was hysterical off camera most of the time this was happening.

In fact, some of the things that you see in the film—like my looking away and trying to keep myself from breaking up—were caused by my looking at Dennis off camera over in the bushes, totally freaked out of his bird, laughing his head off while I'm trying to do my Lyndon Johnson and keep everything together.''

The completely natural, seemingly impromptu nature of that campfire scene has led many observers to assume that the dialogue was improvised. Hopper scotched that rumor, saying, ''all [of] that was totally written.'' And Nicholson corroborated his director, explaining to an interviewer, ''It looks improvised, but most of it was written out in advance. I'd say that, out of everybody in the cast, I stuck closer to the words than anyone—and wound up further away from the character in the script.''

The process of taking George Hanson from the printed page and breathing life into him forced Nicholson to consider who that tragic lawyer was, and what he, the actor, wanted him to be. ''If you read that character in the script, you tended to think of him as a big hick,'' Nicholson explained. ''He seems kind of dumb, not to know what's going on. I didn't want to fall into that cliché. My feeling was that the guy is an imprisoned cat. He's locked up in all this conditioning. He moves away from . . . it. Just like anybody does when they go on a trip. It's the same concept as the drug trip. You get lighter and lighter and freer. There's less interior struggle and you open up. You're suddenly out in open country.

''All these are feelings I've had personally. I wanted to show that he was really a worthwhile person who . . . was being aberrated by the environment. So by the end of it, he was really laying it all out—that freedom was really a very individual thing and that people are frightened of it.''

There was a line of dialogue in the campfire scene when Nicholson said, ''You know, this used to be a hell of a country.'' Fonda was blown away by it. Not long afterward, he would say of Nicholson, ''He really is a patriot. He read that line . . . with an authority that only comes if you believe in it . . . He read it like Henry,'' he added, referring to his father's famous role in *The Grapes of Wrath*. ''He's the Tom Joad, in a way, of our era.''

Once the film was shot, the editing process began, and according to Nicholson, that's where the movie really changed most from the original script. Like the collaborative work that went into the writing, so was there a group effort in the editing. All of the major players were involved, although their memories of who did what sometimes tend to differ. For instance, Nicholson told an interviewer, ''I got to edit my own part, so I picked the best shots . . .'' Hopper, however, said, ''Jack did something, but not his own scenes.'' It's not as if Nicholson was attempting to take any undue credit, because he also conceded, ''I put the trip sequence in, which everyone hates so much.''

Regardless of who did what, *Easy Rider* brought Hopper the New Director first prize at the Cannes Film Festival, and Nicholson the Best Supporting Actor awards from both the New York Film Critics Society and the National Society of Film Critics. And he topped it all off with a Best Supporting Actor Oscar nomination. Of the last, Nicholson showed no false humility when he said, ''If I get an Oscar, I won't feel like I've stolen anything.'' When the Academy Awards show had ended, it was more like the Oscar had been stolen from *him*. The award went to a sentimental favorite, Gig Young, for his work in *They Shoot Horses, Don't They?*

Besides awards, there were rewards, as well. Nicholson had been given a relatively modest salary for his work on *Easy Rider,* but after the movie became a huge hit, BBS showed their appreciation not only for his acting job, but for bringing the project their way and keeping it on track; they rewarded him with a small percentage of the film's take. That also won Nicholson's loyalty, because he continued to work with the small production company over the next several years. And that worked out for Nicholson, too, because it was that company which gave him *Five*

Easy Pieces, securing his place as a genuine leading man and star.

But *Easy Rider* was the film that made it all possible. Asked what would have happened to him had the role not come his way, he jokingly replied, ''I probably would have a major film studio and be directing several acolytes around like, you know, my group, Flying Wackerama Films.'' Despite the humor, one might almost believe it could have happened that way.

In any event, except for a few notable stumbles, Nicholson consciously parlayed his acting success into more than two decades at the top of the Hollywood heap. The key to his long reign as a movie star can be found in the very nature of his role of George Hanson in *Easy Rider;* he was a bridge between the generations—which he has often essayed in one variation or another ever since. He put it best himself when he said, ''I got myself locked right into the sociological curl—like a surf rider—and I found I could stay right in there, ride this, and cut back against it.''

Finally, *Easy Rider* remains not only a nostalgic reminder of the turbulent 1960s, but also the hope of the future. Imagine them all back again, heading down the highway in a *Son of Easy Rider.* It could happen. After all, Nicholson told an interviewer in 1986, ''Oh, babe, I could do a bike picture'd make so much fuckin' money, I mean, you know, it would change them all back around again. That's the next egg for Fonda and Hopper and me . . . It's just a matter of time.''

CHAPTER 8

Three Directions at Once

WITH THE SUCCESS OF *Easy Rider,* for the first time in his long professional life, Nicholson was in the catbird seat. He was a hot property and he knew it. Given his interests as both a filmmaker and an actor, he had three avenues available to him: He could act in big-budget Hollywood studio films; he could continue to remain a Hollywood outsider by starring in smaller-budgeted independent movies; or he could use his star status to wangle an opportunity to direct his own films.

It was typical of Nicholson that he would choose all three, and do them all during the same year.

At the beginning of the new decade, Nicholson admitted, "I've already overscheduled my work, because I'm inexperienced at having so many offers. There was a time when I would do anything that came along . . . Nobody wanted me. Now it's different."

Different, indeed. All of a sudden, he was asked to audition for a role in the Barbra Streisand vehicle *On a Clear Day You Can See Forever* (1970), a megabudget musical that was being made by one of Hollywood's most famous directors, Vincente Minnelli. With mind-numbing speed, Nicholson went from appearing in his usual grade-Z films, which played on the bottom half of drive-in movie double features, to working with the man who shot such classics as *Meet Me in St. Louis* (1944), *An American in Paris* (1951), and *The Band Wagon* (1953).

Many people who've seen *On a Clear Day You Can See Forever* don't realize or remember that Nicholson was in it. His part was that unimpressive. For that matter, so was the movie. That the film flopped badly was less a strike against Nicholson than the fact that he was in it at all. He seemed totally out of place, providing the movie with an ersatz Hollywood image of a hippie that was laughable, if not embarrassing.

The idea of casting someone who might have the pull to bring the younger crowd into movie theaters must have seemed like a good notion at the time. The only problem was that Nicholson's role was unimaginatively shoehorned into the script.

Curiously, the part originally came his way not because of his success in *Easy Rider,* but rather because the aging director had screened *Psych-Out* to find some interesting new lighting effects, and instead, found himself impressed with Nicholson. ("Boy, I'd like to make a movie of Vincente Minnelli watching *Psych-Out*, man," said Nicholson.) Of course, the actor's emergence in *Easy Rider* made his actual casting far more likely.

Nicholson later described his first encounter with the great director, saying, "[it was] just me and him in the room, a cappella, me singing 'Don't Blame Me' to Vincente Minnelli . . . It blew my mind."

While Minnelli always claimed that he hired Nicholson because he liked his voice, the fact is, the one number Jack sang in the movie was cut from the finished film. In retrospect, he was glad it worked out that way, telling an interviewer, "They had the good sense to leave me on the cutting room floor." Just the same, that would be something worth digging out of the vault someday.

In any event, they clipped more than just the song. They cut his hair (despite the fact that he was playing a hippie!) and they cut his screen time. He forgot his lines in his very first scene with Streisand (now, there's a good start), and appeared in just two scenes in the entire film. Neither scene suggested that he showed the slightest bit of promise. He later told *Time* magazine, "All I am in the movie is bad."

Why did he choose to make *On a Clear Day*? The answer is as complex as Nicholson himself. The allure of being in a lavish studio production after being a Hollywood outsider for so many years had to have its appeal. And after struggling financially for more than a dozen years, the payday offered by a big-budget movie could not be ignored, either. While on the one hand he conceded that he took the job for the money, on the other hand, he wanted very much to be able to have on his credit sheet the fact that he had been in a Vincente Minnelli musical.

In that same year, Nicholson directed his first film, *Drive, He Said* (1970). To those unfamiliar with basketball, the title might have suggested a racing movie. Nicholson has always been a big basketball fan (he's famous for his allegiance to the Los Angeles Lakers), and he used his knowledge of the game, as well as his sharp-eyed view of political action, to make an iconoclastic, if flawed, movie about personal political decisions.

Nicholson nearly cast Richard Dreyfuss (before Dreyfuss became a star) in one of the two main roles, but nothing would have turned this film into a hit.

Not that it's a bad movie, because it isn't. The film's commercial failure is best explained by Nicholson, who confessed, "I actually told Bert [Schneider] before we made the film that I didn't think it would make a nickel. Here it was, the height of the youth movement, and this was going to be a movie critical of youth."

Though Nicholson guessed that the movie wasn't going to be very popular, he never imagined that when shown at the Cannes Film Festival, it would elicit such animosity. The movie was jeered and booed by an incredibly hostile audience. A brawl even broke out in the crowd during the showing. Nicholson told Kathleen Carroll of the *New York Daily News*, "I thought I was Stravinsky for a moment. I had a major riot, but it hurt the picture. It was a [financial] disaster; I knew it was going to set me back."

He was right. When the movie finally opened in the

United States, after a battle with the censors concerning nudity and rough language, the American critics hated it as much as the audience at Cannes.

Despite its initially poor reception, there is much to recommend in *Drive, He Said*. Many believe that the basketball scenes are among the best ever shot, capturing the kinetic energy and flow of this fast-paced, fluid game. More important, as Paul D. Zimmerman of *Newsweek* wrote in a review that noted the movie's failings, "This is Nicholson's film, transformed everywhere by his irreverence, honesty, and energy."

Nicholson's dark view of life in this film may not please moviegoers, but one cannot deny his skill in its presentation, or, for that matter, the courage to bite the youth culture hand that had fed him.

Though he thought "it was a very good first film," Nicholson admitted being "depressed" by its failure. He would eventually direct (and star in) two more critical and commercial flops, *Goin' South* (1979) and the long-awaited sequel to *Chinatown* (1974), *The Two Jakes* (1990).

On a Clear Day and *Drive, He Said* might have wrecked his career before it had a chance to take hold. But there was another film that came out that same year, and it's the movie that secured his place as the alienated hero of our times, turning him into a genuine box-office draw.

That movie was *Five Easy Pieces*.

Unlike *Easy Rider*, which received mixed notices, the critics went wild for *Five Easy Pieces*. Pauline Kael, writing in *The New Yorker*, spoke for many critics when she said, "It is a striking movie—eloquent, important, written and improvised in a clear-hearted American [style] that derives from no other civilization, and describing as if for the first time the nature of the familiar American man who feels he has to keep running because the only good is momentum."

Life's critic, Richard Schickel, wrote that Bobby Dupea was "consummately played by Jack Nicholson, who must now be regarded as one of the few truly gifted movie actors we have." That, too, was a sentiment shared by many. And not just among critics. Audiences loved both the film and its star, turning the movie into a smash hit. Even the Academy of Motion Picture Arts and Sciences recognized the film's excellence, giving it five Oscar nominations, including Best Picture and Best Actor. "I'm voting for myself," Nicholson said, "though I don't expect to win. [George C.] Scott already has it sewn up, whether he likes it or not." He was right: Scott won for *Patton*, and *Five Easy Pieces* won nothing.

The irony of Nicholson's second trip to the Oscar ceremonies was that he agreed to star in *Five Easy Pieces* out of loyalty to old friends. It was not a major studio production with a big budget and lots of flash. He did it because he had promised to do it. Simple as that. "I like to finish what I start," he said. "The only way I've been able to eat all these years is through the help of friends. I figure I owe them something."

So Nicholson went back to his roots to make *Five Easy Pieces*—and in more ways than one. Like *Drive, He Said*, it was a BBS production. But unlike that ill-fated venture, *Five Easy Pieces* had more help behind the cameras from such talented old buddies as director Bob Rafelson (who also coproduced and helped provide the original story) and Carol Eastman as screenwriter (who penned the piece under the name Adrien Joyce and who also cowrote the original story). These were people who were both trustworthy and talented. Having worked with Nicholson during the long, lean years, they also knew him well enough to use his personality, his history, his style, to best effect, melding Nicholson to Dupea and Dupea to Nicholson. Surrounded by his compadres, Nicholson was his old self again, calling his friends by the nicknames he had given them. Rafelson was "Curly" because his hair curled up in the back, and Eastman was "Speed" because she was such a slow writer.

As Nicholson well knew, speed wasn't the issue; it was

quality. He had plenty of confidence in Eastman to give him what he needed. And she didn't let him down. He told Gene Siskel of the *Chicago Tribune*: "My character in *Five Easy Pieces* was written by a woman who knows me very well. I related the character to that time in my life, which Carol knew about, well before *Easy Rider* when I was doing a lot of second-rate TV and movies . . . So in playing the character, I drew on all the impulses and thoughts I had during those years when I was having no real acceptance."

The use of Nicholson's own life as an inspiration for the film could be seen in several different ways. Take, for instance, the famous scene in which Nicholson tries to order plain wheat toast in a roadside restaurant. The toast, though readily available, is not on the menu, and the waitress refuses to place the order—a metaphor, if you will, for society's blind obedience to rules, no matter how foolish. Nicholson counters by ordering a chicken salad sandwich on wheat toast, and then, item by item, telling her to hold everything (including the chicken between her knees), charge him for the whole sandwich, but bring him the wheat toast. When she refuses, calling him a troublemaker, he goes wild and violently whips everything off the table.

That particular scene was created out of an actual incident in the actor's life. "Years ago, when I was maybe twenty," Nicholson recalled, "I cleared a table that way at Pupi's, a coffee shop on the Sunset Strip. Carol Eastman, the screenwriter . . . and an old friend of mine, knew about the incident. And Bob Rafelson, the director, and I had gone through something like the bit with a 'no substitutions' waitress, although that time I hadn't dumped the dishes. So, knowing me, Carol and Bob just put the two incidents together and into the script."

On a larger scale, Nicholson confessed: "I was playing it [the role of Dupea] as an allegory of my own career." The key phrase that captures the essence of Nicholson's view of his own life (and Dupea's) is in the scene with his father when he says, "I guess you're wondering what happened to me after my auspicious beginnings."

Nicholson also had auspicious beginnings. As a high school senior, he had earned a college scholarship, only to turn it down to try his luck in Hollywood—many must have thought he had made a foolish mistake. He had a starring role in his first film (albeit a seven-thousand-dollar quickie) and thought he was going to be a star, only to subsist on the edges of Hollywood, a virtual unknown, for more than a decade. Perhaps there was a fear, as well, that people would soon begin wondering what had happened to *him* after *his* "auspicious beginnings" when he bombed in *On a Clear Day You Can See Forever* and sensed that the soon-to-be-released *Drive, He Said* was not going to "make a nickel."

Whatever the reason, that scene with his father burned with a searing emotional intensity. On the day it was shot, however, a confrontation erupted between Rafelson and Nicholson. It had been brewing for a long time. The director had been pushing for him to cry as he confesses his failings to his father, but the actor had consistently resisted. For that matter, the entire scene, as it was written, bothered Nicholson. He had crossed out the whole monologue and had scribbled in the margin, "Something else?"

Years later, Nicholson described what happened that day to *New York Times Magazine* writer Ron Rosenbaum: "I'm in conflict with Rafelson . . . He's always afraid I'm going to make the character too tough and too unapproachable for an audience . . . So we were out on the field where we shot it, and I wrote it [the scene] that morning . . . I tried to get it down to the least amount of verbiage. And that phrase, 'auspicious beginnings,' is what I thought the guy was all about . . . On take one, away I went. And I think it was a breakthrough. It was a breakthrough for me as an actor, for actors. I don't think they'd had this level of emotion, really, in almost any male character until that point."

Nicholson cried, and a generation cried with him. Later,

he was asked if he had been thinking of his own father [he still thought John Nicholson was his real dad] when he cried over the lost opportunities of a lifetime. He simply said, "Of course I was."

While moviegoers lined up to see *Five Easy Pieces*, women seemed to line up to meet Nicholson. It was at this point that he gained his new nickname of "Hollywood Johnny," establishing a reputation not only as a major Hollywood actor, but also as one of the sexiest men in L.A.

CHAPTER 9

The Women

NICHOLSON'S REPUTATION AS a lady's man began long before he became a star. With that killer smile and dangerous look in his eyes, he sometimes attracted women who were looking for an "experience." More often, though, he has had his greatest success with the opposite sex because he is such a thoughtful, sympathetic listener. His secret is that he gives a woman his total, undivided attention. When he is with her, she is the center of his world. Of course, when he isn't with her, he might be giving his total, undivided attention to another woman.

After his marriage with Sandra Knight broke up—in part because he felt he couldn't be monogamous—he became involved with the former model and aspiring actress Mimi Machu. She was tall, dark-haired, and attractive. In fact, she looked a little bit like Sandra Knight. For that matter, unlike most movie stars, who seem to fall for the buxom, blond, and blue-eyed types, Nicholson has (with rare exceptions) consistently opted for thin, tall brunettes.

Nicholson met Mimi Machu (stage name I. J. Jefferson) in 1967 when they appeared together in *Hell's Angels on Wheels,* in which she had a small role.

Nicholson has often been compared to Humphrey Bogart, and if one holds to that comparison, then Mimi Machu was Nicholson's version of Bogart's third wife, Mayo Methot. Like the "Battling Bogarts," Nicholson and Machu had a tempestuous romance. It was a rocky relationship, which nonetheless managed to last four long years.

Machu/I. J. Jefferson had small roles in two other Nicholson films, *Psych-Out* and *Head,* but when Nicholson suddenly got hot with *Easy Rider,* the two of them had to find a new balance in their relationship. They tried. But it must have rankled that few (if any) of the media knew who she was when she sat with Jack on the night he won the New York Film Critics Best Supporting Actor award for *Easy Rider.* While his career was on the rise, hers was stillborn. Nonetheless, she was still with him a year later when he was making *Five Easy Pieces.* Except by then, their romance was breaking into a good many more pieces than five, and none of them were easy.

Actress Susan Anspach, who played one of Nicholson's lovers both on- and off-screen during the making of *Five Easy Pieces,* comforted him during this turbulent period. It was, in Anspach's words, "a very strange relationship." What made it odd was that the two of them were playing out their personal drama in much the same way that they were acting it out in the film. "Jack and I had great electricity for each other," she said. "What was in the film is very much what was between us in real life." If there is a difference between what happened on-screen and off, though, it's that in the movie, the character of Rayette (Karen Black) was left pregnant, and in real life it was Anspach.

One hastens to add that there is a controversy over the identity of the father. Anspach never told Nicholson about the child—a boy—until many years later. She claims it's his, although she has never asked for anything from Nicholson by way of child support or even a dinner for old times' sake. She does, however, consistently insist that Nicholson is the father.

How does Nicholson respond?

"She says that all the time. But because of the way she's been toward me, I've never been allowed a real avenue to find out about it. That's her privacy. She's an avant-garde feminist who—when I met her—was proud of the fact that she already had a child whose father no one knew. She didn't mention her second child to me until six or seven years later . . ."

To this day, Nicholson doesn't know for sure if the young man born in the early 1970s is his son or not. But with his usual candor, he did say that he liked "the idea in a certain way" that the boy might, in fact, be his.

Nicholson's reputation with the ladies apparently put the cabosh on his affair with Anspach. "If the world were an island and we'd been totally alone, we'd have been very much in love," the actress said in the early 1970s. "But . . . I didn't trust his relationships with women based on what I'd observed, and I don't think he was very secure with me because of my straightforwardness."

He always lit fires under women, but once he became famous, the women Nicholson attracted became more famous, too. For instance, there was Karen Black, who had a short run at stardom in the early 1970s. They met before either of them were movie stars, but he was already involved with Mimi Machu, and Black had a boyfriend. Later, when she met Jack after a screening of *Easy Rider* (she had a small role as a prostitute but had no scenes with him), Black began to weep in his arms because she so deeply regretted that she hadn't dated him when she had had the chance.

Yet Black did have another chance when she played his girlfriend, Rayette, in *Five Easy Pieces*. Conceding that she was in love with him, she missed her chance again when Nicholson got involved with Susan Anspach.

Unlike Karen Black, actress Candice Bergen became a good deal more intimate with Jack. The daughter of ventriloquist Edgar Bergen (of Charlie McCarthy and Mortimer Snerd fame), Candice came from an old show business family. She had grown up in the laps of famous film stars and represented (to Jack) a link to the glory of old Hollywood. Except Bergen felt lost in the new Hollywood. When they met, neither one of them was quite ready for the other—though that didn't stop them from trying each other on for size. Later, Nicholson would say of Bergen, "There's another helluva girl. I think we were crying on one another's shoulders, both having experienced bad emotional scenes. We were both on the rebound."

Willowy Faye Dunaway, with whom he costarred in *Chinatown*, was yet another one of his romantic encounters. Contrary to expectations, however, their liaison did not occur during the shooting of their hit film; at that particular time, Jack was in the early stages of his new relationship with Anjelica Huston. In a pattern he would repeat with many of his ex-lovers, Nicholson formed a lasting friendship with Dunaway after their affair was over.

Then there was the much-rumored fling with folk singer Joni Mitchell, with whom he spent long hours on the campaign trail drumming up votes for the doomed presidential bid of Senator George McGovern in 1972. Theirs was supposedly a quiet interlude fueled by the passion of a common goal, yet tacitly understood to be limited to the moment at hand.

Nicholson also dated Brooke Hayward, ex-wife of his *Easy Rider* director, costar, and friend Dennis Hopper. Hayward, the daughter of movie star Margaret Sullavan and famed Hollywood agent Leland Hayward, would later write the best-selling book about her parents, *Haywire*. In the early 1970s, however, she was a divorced woman who found a sympathetic soul in Nicholson. But then, Nicholson seemed to be constantly drawn to the ex-wives of Dennis Hopper. How else to explain his love affair with Hopper's then very recent ex-wife, Michelle Phillips? Unlike most of his other flames, Phillips was a beautiful blonde, who also happened to be a former member of the hot 1960s rock group the Mamas and the Papas.

Hopper had been divorced from Brooke Hayward for several years before Nicholson began seeing her. In the case of Phillips, however, the ink was barely dry on the divorce papers before Nicholson zeroed in on the woman with whom he would be involved for the next three years.

The former pop star had lived with Hopper before their ill-fated eight-day (you read that right) marriage. Still, Jack tried to do the right thing.

"[Jack] was concerned about Michelle," recalled Hopper, "and he called me up and asked if his seeing her was going to screw things up, and I said no." Hopper was impressed with the way Nicholson handled the situation. "That's pretty up-front," he admitted.

Nicholson also had an affair with Hopper's third wife, Daria. According to Hopper, that didn't bother him, either. It's unknown if Hopper has introduced Jack to his new, young and beautiful, fourth bride yet.

It was 1970 when Nicholson and Phillips began seeing each other, and everybody began seeing them; they were a hot number on the party circuit. They represented the melding of the movies and rock and roll, and the press ate it up.

Phillips, her rock career down the tubes with the dissolution of her famous singing group, was trying to break into the movies. Meanwhile, Bruce Dern watched his old friend's sexual escapades in the early to mid 1970s and observed, "I think he'd like for Michelle and him to have it all. I think he'd like to just give everything to her." He had serious doubts, however, that their liaison would be a lasting one. He hesitantly pinpointed the possible problem, saying, "I just think there's too big a gap. I don't know whether it's age, or what . . ." The real pressure, he said, was the "big burden . . . that he should have to put her in a movie with him. And it's a big burden for her to not ask him to put her in a movie with him. It's that terrible husband-and-wife relationship with both people being in the business."

Dern knew what he was talking about.

Before Nicholson made *The Last Detail* (1973), he was nearly in a film with Phillips, a movie called *Three-Cornered Circle*, which was to be directed by the late Hal Ashby. It was based on *The Postman Always Rings Twice*, which, of course, Nicholson later made with Jessica Lange. As Ashby later related, the project fell apart due to MGM's interference, but he already had a commitment from Nicholson, and he wanted to get Phillips as costar. "First of all, on one level, she's a much bigger name than they [MGM management] think she is," he explained, "because those people don't know anything about the music business. They really don't . . . Also, because of the relationship between Jack and Michelle, I thought that they would be very exciting together on film. I really thought Michelle had it. I was almost locked into Michelle before we got Jack."

Nicholson and Phillips never did appear on film together. Nor did they continue to live under the same roof; she took up residence in a house next door. Nicholson simply could not stay monogamous. And just as Dern predicted, the relationship began to flounder.

And no wonder: A new influence had entered Nicholson's life. It was in the early 1970s that Jack met and befriended Hollywood's other most eligible bachelor, Warren Beatty. The two actors both happened to be in western Canada at the same time, Nicholson making *Carnal Knowledge,* and Beatty on location for *McCabe and Mrs. Miller.* When the two of them were introduced by a mutual friend, cartoonist/screenwriter Jules Feiffer, Nicholson sized up Beatty and reportedly said, "Now, that's what a movie star is supposed to look like."

They hit it off right away. There was a natural affinity between Nicholson and Beatty: They both had an instinctive understanding that each of them, in his own way, was the equal of the other. In the rarified Hollywood atmosphere of movie stars, finding a genuine compadre with whom one can share one's thoughts and feelings, as well as with whom one can lustily compete, both professionally and personally, on a level playing field, is incredibly rare. They discovered that they had much in common. In addition to the seriousness with which they both viewed their craft, there was also the seriousness with which they both viewed the art of seduction. In short, Nicholson and Beatty were both girl-crazy.

After firming up their friendship back in Hollywood, the two began cutting a wide swath through the female population of Southern California.

Beatty always had the reputation for getting the girls, but Nicholson, in his own devilish way, was more than a match for him. And they were quite competitive when it came to women—perhaps even more so than in their film careers.

Bruce Dern, who clearly knew Nicholson well, could not help but be amused by his friend's cavorting. Dern dryly explained, "He brags about a lot more pussy than he's ever gotten . . . I'd say if you cut half of his pussy in half, you'd have it about right, and still he probably gets more than anybody around. He and Beatty have contests about it. They talk in those terms."

The upshot of all their carousing, besides bedding truckloads of young beauties, was that their friendship led them to star together in a couple of movies. It also led to Michelle Phillips eventually becoming Warren Beatty's girlfriend. Of course, that didn't last very long. Given Beatty's reputation, that was no surprise. Also no surprise was the fact that there were no hard feelings between any of the parties. The passing of Phillips from Nicholson to Beatty was handled with the same grace and good manners as when she had moved from Hopper to Nicholson. Phillips, incidentally, was not the only woman to follow that particular route. Brooke Hayward also moved from Hopper to Nicholson to Beatty.

What does all this say about Nicholson's attitude toward women? On the one hand, he's been called "a male nymphomaniac." On the other, he's been thoroughly honest and has neither made excuses for his behavior nor claimed any glory for all his screwing around. In this otherwise modern, feminist age, he has somehow managed to become a lovable chauvinist rogue. And no doubt he speaks for a lot of men when he espouses his simple credo: "They hate us—we hate them. They're stronger—they're smarter. They don't play fair."

CHAPTER 10

Banned!

WITH THE SUCCESS of *Five Easy Pieces*, Nicholson was truly in a position to pick his projects, a circumstance that has remained the same now for nearly two decades. He got better over the years in choosing his scripts, but even his misfires were rarely ever safe, easy, or obvious. No other modern film actor/star has taken so many risks with his career as has Nicholson. He generally picks his films based on the identity of the director and the challenging nature of his role. Whether the movie has commercial potential or not usually has little bearing on whether he will commit himself to a production. For example, he turned down the Al Pacino role in *The Godfather* (1972) and the Redford role in *The Sting* (1973), knowing full well that they would both be blockbuster hits. He passed on them because "they were not creatively worth my time." The films he chose to make, instead, were occasionally popular but consistently controversial, especially in the early 1970s.

For instance, there was hardly a more hotly discussed movie in 1971 than *Carnal Knowledge*. In this harsh, seriocomic film, Nicholson plays the caddish, womanizing Jonathan, the guy who uses sexual conquest as a substitute for love. In retrospect, it's hard to believe that the screenwriter, Jules Feiffer, didn't want Jack for the role of Jonathan. Feiffer argued that Nicholson, an Irishman from New Jersey, would hardly be convincing as a Jew from the Bronx (as the part was originally written). Mike Nichols fought Feiffer on the casting and finally convinced him to accept Nicholson, and the screenwriter has been thankful ever since.

The movie received generally good reviews. But there were civic leaders who were less than pleased with both the film's title and its subject matter. This is, after all, a movie that is explicitly about sex. For example, Ann-Margret, who turned her career around and won a Best Supporting Actress Oscar nomination for her portrayal of Bobbie in the film, appeared topless on-screen, and Nicholson was shown at the end of the film impotent and attempting to masturbate with the help of a prostitute. Strong stuff. As a result, the state of Georgia banned the movie.

"They're crazy!" declared Nicholson. Although not using those words, the U.S. Supreme Court backed him up on that when, three years later, it found that the movie was not obscene.

Nicholson's performance in *Carnal Knowledge* was electric. *Newsweek*'s Paul D. Zimmerman put it best when he wrote, "Nearly [everyone is] blasted off the screen by Nicholson's power." Nonetheless, his portrayal of such a charmingly loathsome, ultimately pathetic man was too difficult for the Hollywood establishment to endorse, and the actor was bypassed for a much-deserved Oscar nomination.

The intense controversy surrounding *Carnal Knowledge* meant big box office for the film. It also put Nicholson on the women's lib hit list. He was so effective as Jonathan that people believed he was really like the character in the film. "I was in a lot of trouble with women for about three years because of that movie," he later complained.

Many of Nicholson's friends have said he's most like George Hanson from *Easy Rider*: open, expansive, warm, and a little goofy. Others have said that he's more like Bobby Dupea from *Five Easy Pieces*: complex, charming, and unable to fully commit to a woman. Nobody who knows him has said he's the spitting image of Jonathan. Nicholson said that "Jonathan is exactly the opposite [of myself]. I don't think he knows any way to communicate with women beyond screwing them."

Still, Nicholson found the sympathetic soul inside this tragic character and made a convincing case that "Jonathan is the most sensitive character in the picture. He's the one who doesn't recover from the original sexual triangle [between himself and the characters played by Art Garfunkel and former flame Candice Bergen]. He's never able to really trust girls after that."

His interpretation of Jonathan was what made *Carnal Knowledge* compelling and his character rich and textured. It's also why Mike Nichols would later say, "There is James Cagney, Spencer Tracy, Humphrey Bogart, and Henry Fonda. After that, who is there but Jack Nicholson?"

Carnal Knowledge was a risky project strictly because of its content. Nicholson's other 1971 release was risky in virtually every area one could think of. It had a first-time, untried director, an amorphous, uncommercial script, and a very small budget. Except it also had a friend at the helm.

Working with old friends proved to be a smart choice with *Five Easy Pieces,* so Nicholson went that route with old pal Henry Jaglom, joining the cast of *A Safe Place* (1971). Jaglom had acted alongside Nicholson in the BBS production of *Psych-Out* and had edited parts of *Easy Rider.* Jaglom's directorial debut was overlong, unstructured, self-indulgent, yet irritatingly intriguing. What made the film even remotely commercial was Nicholson's name in the cast list. Jaglom said, "[Jack] did me this huge favor of being in my movie, where he charged [director Mike] Nichols whatever he gets, which is a lot of money now, and for me he did it for a color television set."

Nicholson's presence probably brought the film more

media attention than it might have received (even though Orson Welles and Tuesday Weld were also in the picture), but most of it came in the form of bad reviews. In any event, audiences ignored the movie and it quickly disappeared.

There weren't high expectations for *A Safe Place,* but there was much anticipation about the reuniting of Nicholson and Bob Rafelson for the nostalgically titled *The King of Marvin Gardens* (1972). "From the team that brought you *Five Easy Pieces*" came a darkly photographed, slowly paced, Kafkaesque movie that greatly disappointed those who were expecting a more commercial product.

For many who had grown up playing the board game Monopoly, the title *The King of Marvin Gardens* conjured up the image of a rollicking good time, where characters might wheel and deal in the hope of making a fortune. Oddly enough, wheeling and dealing in order to make a killing *is* a significant element of the movie, but it was purposefully written, photographed, and played in such a low-key style that it becomes mere window dressing for the real story, which is a moody character study of two brothers who cannot quite come to terms with each other.

Despite good personal reviews for Nicholson, most critics dismissed the film as an ambitious failure. It had a modest run in the art house market, creating little discussion except for rumblings about Jack Nicholson's eccentric film choices.

He had agreed to take scale for acting in *The King of Marvin Gardens* rather than the substantial salary he might have demanded for a more mainstream movie, once again showing his loyalty to his old friends and his commitment to offbeat, thoughtful filmmaking.

However, he would not be much in demand—even by his friends—if he continued to make films that failed at the box office. "In order to continue to have your choice of roles," he conceded, "you have to have a success every once in a while.'' What he needed was a property that gave him the best of both worlds: something quirky and intelligent that would still appeal to a broad audience. He found it in *The Last Detail*.

CHAPTER 11

"Bad Ass"

NICHOLSON READ THE NOVEL *The Last Detail* when it was in galley proofs. He immediately pictured himself as the book's lead character, Billy "Bad Ass" Buddusky, a salty-tongued sailor full of piss and vinegar. "It's a strong character, but it's also one I knew audiences would immediately like," he said. Buddusky is vulgar, aggressive, and full of swagger. In short, he is a character who dominates every scene he's in—and Nicholson needed and wanted such a showcase for his talents.

He asked his old friend from the B-movie years, Robert Towne, to write a screenplay based on the book. Towne went right to work on it and fashioned a story that was even better than the original novel.

The usually cynical and hard-nosed Nicholson actually wanted the film to be less of a downer at the end. It might be reasonable to speculate that he was afraid the movie might fail, and he couldn't afford another flop after the dismal reactions to *A Safe Place, Drive, He Said,* and *The King of Marvin Gardens.* It had been two years since *Carnal Knowledge,* and he only had one hit as a star before that, *Five Easy Pieces.* He must have been a little edgy. "Buddusky is killed in the book," he told an interviewer. "I was for ending it as the book did; I was taking an easier way out," he admitted. "I know dramatically what a cheat that is . . . and I think the movie might have had a greater commercial success had that been done. Towne felt that was a cheat, so I went along . . ."

Nicholson's interest in the box-office performance of *The Last Detail* makes even more sense when one knows that the actor had negotiated a deal that gave him a percentage of the film's profits. He stood to make a bundle if the movie was a big hit. He was tempted, but his ultimate willingness to back off and stick with the more truthful, if less audience-pleasing, ending makes one sit up and take notice of this man's genuine artistic integrity.

Nicholson was intimately involved in the casting of the film, and therein lies a tale that also illuminates his personality. He not only saw Buddusky as an opportunity for himself, he also saw the "Mule" Mulhall character (the fellow sailor who helps transport their seventeen-year-old charge to prison) as a chance to give an old friend of his, Rupert Crosse, a black actor, a leading role in a major studio production. It was yet another example of Nicholson's sense of loyalty to the people who stuck by him when *he* was a struggling actor. Most significantly, the role of Mulhall was not described in the script as being black. Roles like that were routinely given white actors without any thought of color-blind casting. Nicholson wanted to change that.

Crosse was hired but suddenly disappeared just as the film was to be shot. When he was located, Nicholson was shattered to learn that the man was ill and dying. With the agreement of director Hal Ashby, production was held up for a week in the hope that Crosse might regain his strength and join the cast. He did not recover. Otis Young replaced him at the last possible moment. Later, when the film was nearly complete, Nicholson took Young aside and shook his hand, congratulating him on being the first black actor in Hollywood history to play a character who wasn't necessarily supposed to be black. Nicholson had made it happen.

The Last Detail wowed the critics, but audiences were only mildly enthusiastic. The film did well at the ticket window, but it didn't set the world on fire. Nicholson once said, "I've always heard if you can make them laugh and make them cry, you have a winner." Well, at least he didn't have a loser.

Nicholson's personal notices were as good as, if not better than, those garnered by the movie. Paul D. Zimmerman at *Newsweek* summed up the critical reaction when he wrote, "[Nicholson's] special blend of cockiness and charm keeps us constantly entertained." Yet Nicholson did more than just entertain. He gave a high-wire job of acting, propelling the story forward through the sheer energy of his performance, keeping the sadness that creeps over the film at the end from becoming too heavy. For his own part, Nicholson said, "*Last Detail* was very satisfying . . . I felt I fully realized what I wanted to do in that film."

The Academy of Motion Picture Arts and Sciences agreed with Nicholson, honoring him with his third Oscar nomination for his virtuoso performance as Buddusky. And, again, he lost. That loss certainly cost him a lot of money. A Best Actor Oscar would have added several million dollars to *The Last Detail*'s gross. Not to mention that Nicholson's price per picture would have gone up. The actor told the *Chicago Tribune* that "not getting our own Academy Award hurt real bad. I did it in that movie, that was my best role. How often does one like that come along, one that fits you?" At this early stage of his stardom, he had no way of knowing just how many roles would come his way that everyone would say he was "born" to play. Nevertheless, he soon rationalized away the loss, saying, "I've always said it's the people who are nominated and *don't* win who make the money out of the Oscar phenomenon because it's always on the come for them."

It was a comforting thought, if not an accurate one. In any event, he would remain "on the come" through yet another standout performance in *Chinatown* the following year. Of far greater importance to him, though, was a moment at one of his parties when he met and fell in love with the young and strikingly beautiful Anjelica Huston.

CHAPTER 12

"Do You Sleep
with My Daughter?"

NICHOLSON'S ROMANCES didn't last long after his relationship with Michelle Phillips ended. "Basically," he said, "I still relate to women by trying to please them as if my survival depended on them. In my long-term relationships, I'm always the one that gets left." In 1973, however, he wasn't involved in a long-term relationship. At least not until he threw a party at his Mulholland Drive house in the hills overlooking Los Angeles.

A tall, dark-haired model named Anjelica Huston was there. Models have always appealed to Nicholson. Mimi Machu was a one-time mannequin, as were many of his later flames, including the long-legged and popular Veruschka, and even model-turned-actress Candice Bergen. But Anjelica was more than a model. She was the daughter of the famous director John Huston, and carried herself like the Hollywood royalty that she was. "I saw cla-a-a-ss," Nicholson later said of the moment when he first caught a glimpse of her.

Like many women, Anjelica was drawn to him by his eyes, except she didn't see them as dangerous at all. "They were kind," she later told an interviewer, "and his whole face lit up when he smiled."

She was twenty-two when they met. He was thirty-six. The age difference was never much of a problem between them, though, because Anjelica had already lived a remarkably varied and rich life. She was, despite her age,

70

as sophisticated as Nicholson, if not more so. She had traveled all over the world, made her film debut at the age of seventeen in a starring role directed by her father in *A Walk with Love and Death* (1969), suffered the slings and arrows of outrageously cruel reviews, and had bounced back to become a famous top model thanks to the efforts of photographer Richard Avedon.

Nicholson was attracted not only to her beauty and sophistication, but to her lineage. As reported in Lawrence Grobel's *The Hustons*, ''An old friend of Nicholson's, Sue Barton, recalled when Jack first told her about Anjelica: 'Not only did he think she was superb, but what excited him most of all was that she was John's daughter. He was so thrilled that he, from Neptune, New Jersey, could have captured this princess whose father was John Huston.' ''

The relationship developed quickly. At the time, Huston was not terribly happy with her life, and Nicholson privately took to calling her ''Anjelica the Moan'' because she complained all the time. In warmer moments he had a more affectionate nickname for her. He called her ''Tootie.'' Nicholson also had a nickname—''the Hot Pole''—although there is some doubt as to who gave it to him. He claimed in an interview that she called him that, but Anjelica laughed and said it wasn't so. It may very well be that Nicholson gave himself the nickname. Either way, it was a colorful description for one of Hollywood's most talked about sex machines.

One of the reasons their romance held together during the early years was that ''she's a sensible person,'' according to Nicholson. ''A career is not so important to her. She's not ambitious that way.'' In other words, she wasn't in competition with him, nor was she as professionally needy as some of his other former girlfriends. Unlike his relationships with Mimi Machu and Michelle Phillips, there wasn't the pressure to get her into the movies; she had her own connections through her father. Besides, she wasn't so sure she wanted to be an actress, anyway.

Not long after they began seeing each other, circumstances conspired to land Nicholson the starring role of J. J. (Jake) Gittes in *Chinatown* (1974). In a brilliant bit of casting, Anjelica's father played the villain (Noah Cross) in the hit film. According to Nicholson, "One of the secrets of *Chinatown* is that there was a kind of triangular offstage situation. I had just started going with John Huston's daughter, which the world might not have been aware of, but it actually fed the moment-to-moment reality of my scene with John."

In the movie, Nicholson has an affair with Cross's daughter, Evelyn (Faye Dunaway) and is confronted by Cross/Huston, who says, "Mr. Gittes . . . do you sleep with my daughter? Come, come, you don't have to think about it to remember." According to the director, Roman Polanski, "The only time that Anjelica came to visit us on the set was that scene . . . She turned and walked away. She laughed later and told me that she was a bit embarrassed."

Anjelica might have felt awkward, but Nicholson and the elder Huston did not. The two hit it off from the very start and, over the years, became rather close. At one point, Huston even reportedly suggested to his daughter that "we marry this man."

In *Chinatown,* fueled by their mutual respect and the expert directing of Polanski, Nicholson and Huston, as well as Dunaway, gave exciting and truly memorable performances.

But it easily might never have happened.

One of those ineffable, fortuitous—or perhaps intuitive—decisions that can change a career took place in the months leading up to the making of what became the most important Nicholson film to date. On the surface, the role of J. J. Gittes, a romantic leading man, did not fit the Nicholson mold. He was really a character star, and the casting was not immediately obvious. On the other hand, he seemed born to play the part of Jay Gatsby, the mysterious self-made man, in the Paramount production of

The Great Gatsby (1974). In fact, studio chief Robert
Evans had offered him the role of Gatsby. Evans said,
"Jack wanted a lot of money to play the part, and he
wanted to play it badly; we just couldn't afford him."
Instead, Robert Redford got the role, only to see the film
massacred by the critics. Score one for Nicholson pricing
himself out of the market.

Evans still wanted to work with the actor, however, and
it came about because Robert Towne had an itch to write
something original for Nicholson. Evans, therefore, got to
Nicholson by virtue of commissioning the screenwriter of
The Last Detail to pen a script that became *Chinatown*.

Loosely based on the real-life 1908 Owen Valley Scandal in Los Angeles, *Chinatown* was a re-creation of the
film noir style of the 1940s. In terms of its tone and content, though, it was something much more. The movie
was a contemporary allegory about modern corruption in
high places (e.g., Watergate). Chinatown, as a symbol,
was used in the film to represent a moral and ethical
quicksand in which modern society is sinking. Gittes is
told, with a shrug, to quit fighting, that there's nothing he
can do. After all, "It's Chinatown." In this same respect,
the film was also a signpost of the moral confusion of the
Vietnam war era, an echo of the American soldiers' cynical credo, "It don't mean nothin'."

Nicholson was slated to play J. J. Gittes from the very
beginning. The heavy favorite for the female lead (Evelyn
Mulwray) was Robert Evans's wife, actress Ali McGraw.
After she ran off with Steve McQueen, however, any
chance she had of playing John Huston's daughter and Jack
Nicholson's lover in the film were effectively reduced to
zero. Faye Dunaway was Evans's second choice to play
the role, and she jumped at the opportunity.

When it came time to cast some of the lesser parts,
Roman Polanski chose himself to play the vicious hood-
lum who slices Gittes's nose. He was memorably ferret-
like, and the scene was much-discussed for its violence.
Another result of the nose-cutting scene was that Nichol-

son had to wear a big, clumsy bandage on his nose for more than half the picture. This, too, was Polanski's idea, and Nicholson went along with it. (It has often been observed that few stars would have allowed themselves to be filmed that way.) There were fights between Nicholson and Polanski—but not on the issue of the bandage. Although there was one fight that did have something to with his nose . . .

Nicholson had borrowed a TV set to watch a Los Angeles Lakers playoff game. The fanatical Lakers fan was watching it in his dressing room when the call came from the set that his nose was needed for a difficult shot. "I suppose I *might* have put a little pressure on the situation, but Roman had a little camera problem and he could get impatient."

The actor, anxious to get back to watching the game, was apparently riding Polanski about the delay. Suddenly the director "wrapped" the shot, despite the fact it clearly hadn't been finished. "I reached up and ripped the lighting out and said, 'You're right, that is a wrap,'" recalled Nicholson. "Now they couldn't set it up again. Roman ran into my dressing room, grabbed the television, and smashed it on the floor."

The scene escalated still further.

Nicholson tore off his costume, got into his car, and sped away. Polanski also drove away in a huff. By chance, a short while later, the two men spotted each other and couldn't help but laugh about the entire episode. Peace was restored.

Despite their occasional differences, Nicholson and Polanski developed a mutual respect and became rather good friends. Their relationship was solid enough for Nicholson to joke roughly about the director, saying, "[Polanski's] an irritating person whether he's making a movie or not making a movie."

Polanski was more than irritating to Robert Towne. In an ironic reversal, Towne, who had insisted on the more dour ending for *The Last Detail*, thought that Polanksi made the ending of *Chinatown* too "relentlessly bleak." In the first draft, the Huston character is killed by his daughter, who, with Gittes's help, flees the country with her sister/daughter. In the final version, the Faye Dunaway character is killed, and the child she bore with her father is taken away by Huston as Nicholson looks on helplessly.

The movie, as ultimately shot, was an exploration of evil by Polanski, who was still coming to terms with the brutal and senseless slaying of his pregnant actress wife, Sharon Tate, at the hands of Charles Manson and his followers. Or, as Ron Rosenbaum of the *New York Times* said of the movie's final scene: "The shattering discovery Gittes makes at the end—that beneath the deepest levels of political corruption is something even darker and more frightening, the ineradicable corruption of the human heart—gave that 1974 film the added dimension of being a kind of farewell to arms for '60s idealism."

When *Chinatown* was shown for the first time to the cast and crew in its rough-cut form, everyone knew they had a winner. Nicholson reportedly turned to Robert Evans and said, "Mogul, we got that hot one. Get those checks ready—we're on our way."

Were they ever.

Time magazine's Jay Cocks called *Chinatown* an "exotic and cunning entertainment." Paul Zimmerman, over at *Newsweek*, trumpeted the film as "spellbinding . . . a brilliant cinematic poem in the style of Poe circa 1974, a highly atmospheric portrait of evil-doing promoted by official power and big money, and unchecked by the agencies of law enforcement—Watergate with real water."

Nicholson had been flirting with superstardom, and *Chinatown* put him over the top. Critics called him everything from "Bogart in the age of rock and roll" to "one of the smartest actors around." His producer, Robert Evans, put Nicholson's success in context: *"[Chinatown]* establishes him as a major box-office star, which he hadn't been until *Chinatown* came out. He was an important critical star, and he had his coterie of fans, but now *China-*

town is a breakthrough picture. It's a very important picture to Jack, as evidenced by his being on the cover of *Time* magazine.''

The attention didn't stop there. Nicholson was again nominated for a Best Actor Academy Award. It was his fourth nomination, and this one looked like a winner. The *New York Daily News* said, ''Not since Ray Milland guzzled his way to an Oscar in *The Lost Weekend* has an actor been such a sure bet as Jack Nicholson.'' The article went on to quote ''one well-known beauty'' who opined, ''If only half the actresses with whom he's had affairs vote for him, he'll win by their ballots alone.'' It was not to be. He suffered his fourth loss as Art Carney took the Best Actor Oscar for *Harry and Tonto*.

Nicholson was beginning to chafe under the label of perennial loser. ''Maybe [the next year] I'll be the sentimental favorite,'' he said.

Sentiment would have nothing to do with it.

CHAPTER 13

1975—A Cuckoo Year

IN 1975 NICHOLSON PUT ON a display of remarkable versatility. He was the enigmatic star of Michelangelo Antonioni's *The Passenger,* gave an adroit comic performance in *The Fortune,* sang a song in the film version of the rock opera *Tommy,* and capped the year with his Academy Award–winning portrayal of Randle McMurphy in the megahit *One Flew Over the Cuckoo's Nest.* From esoteric artiness to broad farce, and then from a musical to a bigger-than-life dramatic performance, Nicholson showed not only a tremendous acting range, he also forcefully demonstrated his continued willingness to do the unexpected, to stretch himself, to take dangerous chances.

After all, why would a Hollywood superstar, fresh from a triumph in a film like *Chinatown,* choose to go to Europe and star in a painfully slow, brooding intellectual exercise in ennui such as *The Passenger?* If you are Jack Nicholson, you do it because you "want to act in . . . films that have some kind of meaning to me."

If you are Jack Nicholson, you also want to work with the cinema's most illustrious directors. Antonioni had made such internationally acclaimed films as *L'Avventura* (1960), *La Notte* (1961), and *Blow Up* (1966). Collaborating on a movie with a director who made films that were admired by the intelligentsia had a strong appeal to an actor who didn't want to be considered a mere Hollywood film personality.

So off he went to Europe. Anjelica came along, as well,

getting some modeling assignments so she could be with him. It was tough keeping up. Originally entitled *Profession: Reporter,* the movie was shot in London, Munich, Barcelona, Almeria, and the Sahara Desert.

When the movie opened, critics were divided. Some thought the film brilliant, others dismissed it as muddled and ponderous. On a personal level, however, Nicholson escaped with generally good reviews in a movie that did not last long in the theaters.

The contrast between *The Passenger* and *The Fortune* could not have been greater. While *The Passenger* was intended for the art house circuit, *The Fortune* was aimed at the huge mass market. The latter film was a Hollywood comic farce that had every surefire ingredient one could imagine. Start with the blockbuster cast: two of the hottest actors in the business in the same film, Warren Beatty and Jack Nicholson. Then there was the industry's much-admired director of comedies, Mike Nichols. And finally, there was a script by the ever faithful and talented Carol Eastman, writing again as Adrien Joyce.

It was a bomb.

What went wrong? Start with a bad script. A comedy has to be funny, and this was, in its own way, as plodding as *The Passenger.* If the movie had a saving grace, it was Nicholson's acting riff as Oscar (a prescient name, if ever there was one). Though it was damned by the critics, who called *The Fortune* creatively bankrupt, many still managed to applaud Nicholson's efforts. Leonard Maltin, for one, said of the film that it was "worth seeing if only for Nicholson's wonderful comic performance."

The actor enhanced his portrayal with a wickedly funny hairdo that looked something like Larry Fine's from the Three Stooges. When asked by an interviewer if looking bad on-screen bothered him, he replied, "I'm not without vanity. But I don't want any characteristic of mine to overlap into the character . . . If someone's going to cut up your nose, you'll have to walk around with a bandage. In

Fortune, having a kinky-headed character be kinky-headed is a good visualization.''

The Fortune fared no better with audiences than it did with the critics. At least one member of the Nicholson household, however, could count herself lucky. Jack had wanted Anjelica to test for the female lead (played by Stockard Channing), but she didn't want to do it. He must have been impressed with her strength of character; how many actors would turn down a chance to star in a Mike Nichols film, with the star power of Nicholson and Beatty seemingly providing a surefire hit?

While Nicholson was trying to get his present girlfriend into the movie, his buddy Warren was trying to get Nicholson's former live-in girlfriend, Michelle Phillips, into a serious relationship. ''Warren's high school principal parents would've been proud of the way it was handled,'' Nicholson later told Nancy Collins of *Rolling Stone*. ''Michelle, being the lady she is, took the trouble to call and ask if I had any feelings about them, which I did: I thought it was fabulous, because I like them both very much. Michelle's a real stand-up woman. You can't *get* her to do a dishonorable thing. And . . . can she move it!''

Joining an all-star cast in Ken Russell's version of the rock opera *Tommy,* Nicholson did a short turn as the Doctor. Based on the hit album by The Who, the film told its story of the redemption of a ''deaf, dumb, and blind kid'' (Roger Daltry) strictly through the use of rock and roll. There was virtually no dialogue in the movie. In other words, Nicholson had to sing.

Unlike his experience in *On a Clear Day You Can See Forever,* this time his song did not end up on the cutting room floor. Mind you, he was no Elton John (who played the Pinball Wizard), but he was credible, and more to the point, what difference did it make? The whole movie could hardly be taken seriously. It was a typical Ken Russell overindulgence, full of pointless visual chicanery. At best, empty-headed fun, at worst, an excessive and insulting movie, *Tommy* was nonetheless successful at the box office.

Nicholson's reason for his cameo appearance in the film? "I thought it might be fun to do a Russell picture." Perhaps the flashy exuberance of Russell's filmmaking somehow counterbalanced the bleak spareness of Antonioni's. Happily, he has avoided either such excess ever since.

It would have been an eccentric, perhaps somewhat disappointing, 1975 had *The Passenger, The Fortune,* and *Tommy* been the full extent of Nicholson's work that year. Add *One Flew Over the Cuckoo's Nest* to the mix, however, and it becomes an even more fascinating and brilliant twelve months—arguably the most multifaceted expression of his talent during his entire career.

One Flew Over the Cuckoo's Nest was a best-selling novel when it was published in 1962. Kirk Douglas bought the dramatic rights to the book before it hit the stands and turned it into a play. It opened on Broadway in 1963 with Douglas in the starring role of Randle McMurphy, but was a surprising flop. Despite that setback, the play continued to get mounted on stages all over the world while Douglas valiantly tried to get the funding to turn the property into a movie. The conventional wisdom was that the story was too much a mental reverie by the book's narrator, Chief Bromden, to make a successful transition to the screen. The funding was not forthcoming.

Years passed. Douglas became too old for the part, and the women's movement took its toll on the novel. Big Nurse, as portrayed in the book, was a mechanistic, totally evil creature. Women's groups would not have stood for such a character by the mid-1970s. When Kirk Douglas turned the project over to his son, Michael, whose acting career was then stalled, things suddenly began to happen.

Michael and his producing partner, Saul Zaentz, first hired Kesey to write a new script for ten thousand dollars.

They also hired Milos Forman, who had built a strong reputation as a director in Czechoslovakia with such films as *The Firemen's Ball* (1967) and had managed the transition to Hollywood with *Taking Off* (1971).

Now that Douglas and his partner had a script and a director, they needed a cast. In particular, they needed their Randle McMurphy.

Happily, there was an open channel between producer and star. "Michael Douglas talked to me early on about *One Flew Over the Cuckoo's Nest*," Anjelica Huston told an interviewer. "I don't know if I was the instrumental factor in that, but I mentioned to Jack that Michael wanted to see him about it."

Douglas and Nicholson met, talked, and struck a deal. Each of them was enormously pleased with the terms of their agreement. As a producer, Douglas had to be especially thrilled that he had snared the one actor everyone in Hollywood said was a natural for the role. Landing Nicholson changed the film's commercial prospects dramatically. As a result, Douglas and Zaentz immediately doubled their budget from $1.5 million to $3 million.

On first blush, it might be reasonable to assume that they had to increase their budget to pay Nicholson's salary. Blush again. Nicholson agreed to star in the film with *no* up-front salary or guarantee. Instead, he agreed to play Randle McMurphy for a big slice of the gross. It was a gutsy business decision on the actor's part. If the film flopped, he would have worked for virtually nothing. Why did he decide to structure the deal that way? His old friend, *Chinatown* producer Bob Evans, related a story Nicholson told him: "Bob," said Nicholson, "I was in New York last year, and I saw an NYU student version of *Cuckoo's Nest*. At the end they all stood up and applauded, went wild. Now, if they're gonna applaud it with students doing it, I want to *own* this movie."

Nicholson had long been aware of *Cuckoo's Nest*. "When I first read the book, I thought McMurphy would be a fabulous part for any actor,'' he said. ''I was too young for it then, but when it came around this time, I was ready.'' Well, almost ready.

Nicholson didn't see McMurphy the same way most everyone else did. ''I could name you five guys in Hollywood who are more right for this part than I am,'' he claimed during the film's shooting. Later, he would explain what finally motivated him to take the role, despite some serious misgivings. ''The starting problem with *Cuckoo's Nest* was that everybody thought that I was born to play the part, and in my mind it was a part that was going to be very difficult for me to play. So I felt like, jeez, they already think I'm supposed to be great in this, and I'm not so sure. And really, that anxiety was almost the main motivation for doing the part. I wanted to allay it, ya know? I wanted to put it aside. I usually follow my fears in that area. I have to. It's real easy to get comfortable as an actor.''

During the preproduction process, while actors were being hired, the script went through a major metamorphosis. The producers rejected Kesey's version of the screenplay, and they hired Lawrence Hauben and Bo Goldman to rewrite it. According to Nicholson, however, it was Milos Forman who ''solved the script.'' With his direction, everyone finally had what they wanted: a story that was not so much a battle between an old-fashioned, virile man and a vicious, castrating (or lobotomizing) woman, but a clash between two very strong-willed people who only happen to be a man and a woman. As a consequence of that change, the story also became more focused on the larger theme of personal freedom versus institutional order—a distinctly American (and very commercial) conflict.

The next hurdle was finding the actress who would play Nurse Ratched. As the process dragged on, Nicholson became incensed and later vented his frustration, saying, ''I can't tell you the actresses that turned Nurse Ratched down. [But we can: Among them were Faye Dunaway, Anne Bancroft, Jane Fonda, and Ellen Burstyn.] I'm very disappointed. One area where I'm not sympathetic with the feminist movement is as actresses. They do scream for roles for women—or *we* do—and here's one of the great roles for women, and a lot of people turned it down. They didn't want to play heavies. You would *not* get that response from actors. This role would not be turned down by several actors because of that reason. An actor should never care.'' Louise Fletcher, an actress with very little movie experience, eventually won the part of Nurse Ratched (and, eventually, an Oscar for her performance).

In order to get the feeling of the mental hospital setting, Nicholson and the cast rehearsed for two weeks at the Oregon state mental hospital in Salem, where the movie was largely shot. ''If you really wanted to get into the research, you could always go upstairs before any scene and check it out,'' said Nicholson.

Even after the filming began, however, the actor was still unsure of his characterization. ''I don't quite have McMurphy down yet,'' he conceded to an interviewer. ''I'm still playing my own quality.''

Soon thereafter he found the key to McMurphy, and later explained it by saying, ''This guy's a scamp who knows he's irresistible to women, and in reality he expects Nurse Ratched to be seduced by him. This is his tragic flaw. This is why he ultimately fails. I discussed this with Louise [Fletcher]. I discussed it only with her. That's what I felt was actually happening with that character—it was one long, unsuccessful seduction which the guy was so pathologically sure of.''

Milos Forman put it succinctly when he said of the McMurphy character, ''You don't know if he's a nut or a hero.'' In actual fact, he was both.

Though now considered one of the great films of the 1970s, *Cuckoo's Nest* didn't fare all that well with the critics when it first opened. Many compared it unfavorably with the novel, while others carped at its supposedly simplistic message. Strangely, even as they attacked it, they generally admitted that it was a powerful, well-crafted movie. And there was an avalanche of praise for Nicholson. As Jack Kroll of *Newsweek* proclaimed, "McMurphy is the ultimate Nicholson performance—the last angry crazy profane wise-guy rebel, blowing himself up in the shrapnel of his own liberating laughter."

The critics were wrong about *Cuckoo's Nest* and right about Nicholson. In any event, audiences decided for themselves about the merits of the movie by voting at the ticket window, plunking down a staggering $125 million to see the movie, and in the process, making Nicholson a very rich man thanks to his profit-sharing deal with the producers.

For the fifth time since 1969 and for the third year in a row, Nicholson was being touted for an Oscar. He was beginning to wonder if he'd ever win. Talk of his four previous failures, however, tended to annoy him. "After you've been chosen one of the five best actors of the year—and there are only about forty thousand—then people come up to you and ask how it felt to lose. One doesn't lose an Academy Award," he told a reporter.

There are actors who have turned their noses up at the whole notion of Academy Awards. Famous examples abound, including George C. Scott and Marlon Brando. Nicholson doesn't feel that way. On the one hand, he has readily admitted that the Oscars are "a promotional device." On the other, he has forthrightly conceded to reporter Jerry Parker, "[The Oscars have] had a very positive effect on me, and I've tried to reciprocate by spending about sixteen of the most uncomfortable hours of my life attending the ceremonies. I don't like the idea of going, but I've gone out of a sense of fair play."

There was nothing uncomfortable about the ceremonies honoring Hollywood's best of 1975. Nicholson, of course, had his fifth nomination, as expected. But this time there was no denying his scintillating performance. He won the Best Actor Oscar and certainly was one of the major reasons that *Cuckoo's Nest* became the first movie to sweep all five top Academy Awards since *It Happened One Night*

A portrait of a genuinely fun-loving star whose shades are as omnipresent as his mischievous expressions. (Photo by Frank Edwards, © Fotos International)

Nominated for Best Supporting Actor for *Easy Rider* (1969), Jack stops
his director, Dennis Hopper, on Oscar night. Looking on with
ever-increasing interest is Hopper's wife, singer Michelle Phillips, of
the 1960s rock group, the Mamas and the Papas, who would later
divorce Hopper and move in with Nicholson. (Photo by
Frank Edwards, © Fotos International)

(Opposite):
Though Jack lost his first bid for an Oscar, he clearly enjoyed his talk
with superstar Barbra Streisand during the 1970 Academy Award
dinner. He certainly seems more comfortable with Streisand here than
he did on-screen with her in *On a Clear Day You Can See Forever*
(1970). (Photo by Frank Edwards, © Fotos International)

Nicholson met actress Candice Bergen long before they starred together in *Carnal Knowledge* (1971). Here they are at the premiere party for Liza Minnelli's *Sterile Cuckoo* (1969). There was, however, nothing sterile about the relationship between Jack and Candice. (Photo by Frank Edwards, © Fotos International)

Clean shaven and brandishing his 1000-watt smile, Nicholson is seen here in 1972 with Dennis Hopper's ex-wife, Brooke Hayward, daughter of famed agent Leland Hayward and actress Margaret Sullivan. He obviously likes Hopper's taste in women. Tagging along is "Mama" Cass Elliot of the Mamas and the Papas (keeping an eye on Jack for her friend, Michelle?). (Photo by Frank Edwards, © Fotos International)

So civilized. Though their long-term affair was over, Jack and Michelle Phillips had only smiles for each other when they met at an opening in 1974. By this time, Michelle had gone on to have an affair with Nicholson's good buddy, Warren Beatty. (Photo by Frank Edwards, © Fotos International)

Nicholson deeply resented never getting the chance to audition for Dustin Hoffman's role in Mike Nichols' *The Graduate* (1967). However, Jack and Mike eventually became good friends, collaborating on three films. They are seen here at a 1972 fundraising concert for presidential candidate George McGovern at New York's Madison Square Garden. (© Mark Sherman, Pictorial Parade, Inc.)

Jack Nicholson and Faye Dunaway in a scene from *Chinatown* (1974), the movie that turned Jack into a romantic leading man. Romantic, indeed. Some say that Dunaway shared Jack's bed offscreen as well as on. (Photo courtesy of Pictorial Parade)

Nicholson achieved tinsel-town immortality in 1974 when he added his footprints and handprints to those of his illustrious peers at the famous Chinese Theater in Hollywood. And many of his greatest roles were all still ahead of him. (Photo by Frank Edwards, © Fotos International)

Old and new Hollywood meet at the Oscars in April of 1975, as Jack shakes hands with the legendary Fred Astaire. For Nicholson, a longtime film fan, it was a moment to treasure. Admiring Nicholson in his rakish beret is Astaire's daughter, Ava. (Photo by Frank Edwards, © Fotos International)

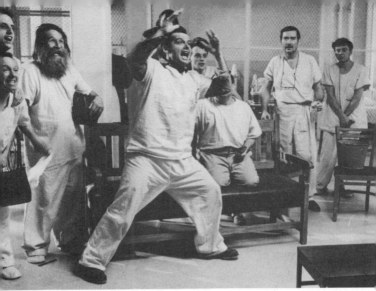

Nicholson's long-time lover, Anjelica Huston, paved the way behind the scenes for Jack's most famous role of the 1970s—Randle McMurphy in *One Flew Over the Cuckoo's Nest* (1975). (Photo courtesy of Pictorial Parade)

Seen here in a still from *Tommy* (1975), Nicholson is reunited with the beautiful Ann-Margret, with whom he previously starred in *Carnal Knowledge*. She may be one of the few stars he bedded only on film. (Photo courtesy of Fotos International)

After four tries, Nicholson finally took home the Best Actor Oscar for his work in *One Flew Over the Cuckoo's Nest*. But he's also smiling because he wisely chose to take no salary for his acting job in the film, opting instead for a big chunk of the profits—of which there were millions upon millions. (Photo by Frank Edwards, © Fotos International)

The heavyweight acting match in *Missouri Breaks* (1976) was a knockout for Nicholson's idol, Marlon Brando, who played the bad guy and stole the movie outright. But Jack learned a valuable lesson: The villain gets the showy scenes. No wonder Nicholson would later burn up the big screen in such wonderfully villainous showcases as *The Shining* (1980), *The Witches of Eastwick* (1987), and *Batman* (1989). (Photo courtesy of Fotos International)

Nicholson and Anjelica Huston, seen here during happier times, have been Hollywood's most enduring unmarried couple. She called him "The Hot Pole." But Jack's highly publicized affair with a British actress and his fathering of a child with yet another woman have certainly cooled things off. (Photo by Frank Edwards, © Fotos International)

While it is generally understood that Anjelica tolerated Jack's affairs with other women, there are many who believe that his public humiliation of her may destroy the great love of his life—a love quite evident in the playfulness of the moment captured here. (© Tim Boxer, Pictorial Parade)

Nicholson is a social animal, hardly a reclusive star. For instance, he is seen here with singer/actress Bette Midler at a fundraising party for the Equal Rights Amendment. (Photo by Frank Edwards, © Fotos International)

Who could resist that killer smile? Nicholson flashed it at Oscar's 50th anniversary in April, 1978. Seen with him are screen legend Janet Gaynor along with Diane Keaton, who won the Best Actress Oscar for *Annie Hall*. Later Nicholson would nearly make a fool of himself over Keaton on the set of *Reds* (1981). (Photo by Frank Edwards, © Fotos International)

Ham for dinner? Nicholson directs himself in *Goin' South* (1978), a wonderfully goofy flop. It was his last directorial effort before the heralded release of the far more serious opus, *The Two Jakes* (1990). (Photo courtesy of Pictorial Parade)

Nicholson's daughter, Jenny, was born in 1963 and he has always been very protective of her. Raised by her mother, Sandra Knight, she lived in Hawaii outside the glare of public scrutiny. Jack's regret is that he spent far too little time with her when she was growing up. (Photo by Frank Edwards, © Fotos International)

Looking tough, Nicholson is caught here at the Roxy in Los Angeles, sporting the moustache he would wear in both *Reds* (1981) and *The Border* (1981). (Photo by Frank Edwards, © Fotos International)

Nicholson knows what it means to be an outsider, so it was with deep
feeling that he took part in honoring longtime Hollywood exile
Orson Welles in 1981 at a tribute for the actor/director at the Beverly
Hilton Hotel. Also at the table is Jack's actress friend, Joan Hackett.
(Photo by Frank Edwards, © Fotos International)

Debra Winger casts a longing glance in Nicholson's direction in this
publicity still for *Terms of Endearment* (1983). But it was with
Shirley MacLaine that Nicholson had all his big scenes, in a movie that
is considered a major turning point in Jack's career. (Photo courtesy of
Fotos International)

April 9, 1984, was a big night at the Oscars for *Terms of Endearment*.
Jack won his second Academy Award, this one for Best Supporting
Actor. Nicholson played a middle-aged lothario with a sagging
stomach, winning the hearts of the critics as well as that of
Shirley MacLaine, who took top honors with a Best Actress Academy
Award. (Photo by Frank Edwards, © Fotos International)

Nicholson doesn't look too happy about being captured on film during a
sentimental journey back to his old haunts near Neptune City,
New Jersey. (© Frank Mastro, Pictorial Parade)

Seen here surrounded by his beautiful co-stars, Cher, Susan Sarandon, and Michelle Pfeiffer, Nicholson was at his devilish best in *The Witches of Eastwick* (1987). Of the casting, Cher said that "[Nicholson] was like the jewel and we women were the setting." (Photo courtesy of Pictorial Parade)

Nicholson, known among friends by such nicknames as "Mr. Cafe Society" and "Hollywood Johnny," became known to a whole new generation of fans as "The Joker." After more than twenty years of stardom and love affairs with many of the world's most beautiful women, he has even more reason to be smiling now. (Photo © Frank Spooner) in 1934. In addition to Nicholson's Oscar, the film won for Best Screenplay, Best Actress, Best Director, and Best Picture. It was a high point in Nicholson's career. Times would not be this good again for quite a while.

CHAPTER 14

Troubles and Disappointments

WHEN NICHOLSON WAS OFFERED a small role in *The Last Tycoon* (1976), he leaped at the opportunity to work with the legendary director Elia Kazan, for probably the same reason he jumped at the chance to work with Vincente Minnelli and Michelangelo Antonioni: He wanted to be associated with the great names of film history. There were plenty of great names to go around. *The Last Tycoon* was produced by the famous Sam Spiegel, the screenplay was penned by the illustrious Harold Pinter, and the film was based on an unfinished work by literary giant F. Scott Fitzgerald.

Nicholson had a role that has been described as a cameo, but it's really more important than that. He played a communist labor organizer named Brimmer, and in his few minutes on-screen, he had an electric effect, jump-starting what was, frankly, a rather dull movie.

The film was treated respectfully by the critics, but with very little passion. As Jack Kroll of *Newsweek* magazine so aptly put it, ''It's an exceptionally well-made movie. But something is missing . . . a certain vital incandescent fusion of style and feeling.'' The only thing incandescent in the movie was Nicholson. Truth to tell, he picked one of the best parts in the film, and he was rewarded by a slew of good notices. In addition, by virtue of his small role, he lost no luster in his standing as one of the two biggest stars in Hollywood—DeNiro, the lead of *The Last*

Tycoon, being the other—when the film stumbled badly at the ticket windows. On the contrary, Nicholson's willingness to take a modest role (and a backseat to DeNiro) showed him to be a fully confident star who was more interested in good roles than in fame.

His good reviews, however, didn't help turn the film into a winner. Considering its pedigreed production people and sterling cast (the film also boasted Robert Mitchum, Jeanne Moreau, Ingrid Boulting, Tony Curtis, Donald Pleasence, Ray Milland, Dana Andrews, and Theresa Russell), the movie's failure had to have been a shock to the producing company, Paramount Pictures.

There were other shocks to come, but they were for Nicholson. And they were no one's fault but his own.

Nicholson had finished filming his small role in *The Last Tycoon* and was busy during the early months of 1976 promoting *One Flew Over the Cuckoo's Nest*. Anjelica Huston also had a role in *Tycoon*, albeit a tinier one, and she had stayed behind in Los Angeles in order to complete her scenes.

On the road in New York, Nicholson began seeing other women—some of whom Anjelica apparently knew personally. Nicholson was fully aware of the consequences of his actions. He confided in a friend, "I think I may have started a few brushfires in New York that could burn all the way to the coast." He was right. A raging fire of hurt and indignation had seared Anjelica. She set up housekeeping in her own apartment and began dating Nicholson's pal Ryan O'Neal. It might not have been intended as tit for tat, but that was the net result.

When Nicholson returned to the coast, the two patched things up, and she was on his arm the night he won the Oscar for *Cuckoo's Nest*. It didn't last. They broke up again a short while later, and this time she moved into O'Neal's Malibu home.

Looking back to that time, Nicholson said, "I didn't blame her in the beginning. I didn't like it, but I think being my girlfriend has so many things even I couldn't deal with that I can honestly say I don't blame her, although I was hurt.

Their breakup was more complicated than most. Besides the personal pain and disappointment that they shared, Anjelica suddenly and inexplicably found herself involved in the infamous Roman Polanski rape case.

She had gone to Nicholson's house on Mulholland Drive, gathering some of her belongings to take to O'Neal's place. She thought the house was empty. Instead, she stumbled upon Nicholson's houseguest, Polanski, and a thirteen-year-old girl named Sandra in the living room. According to Polanski's autobiography, it was rather obvious that he and the young girl had been making love. Later, when the police questioned Anjelica at the house, they found some cocaine in her pocketbook and brought her down to the station. She was granted immunity on the drug charge in exchange for her testimony about Polanski.

It was an ugly situation.

While all this was going on, Nicholson was in Aspen, Colorado, on a skiing vacation. "When I heard about [Polanski's arrest]," he said, "I was told, 'Don't talk about it. Don't find out anything, don't become involved, since you aren't at all.' And since I never knew what might happen as a result of its being at my residence, I was advised to not communicate, for the good of all concerned. So I know very little about it." Nonetheless, he spoke up loudly and often in Anjelica's defense, claiming that the authorities had no business arresting her in the first place. His position was proved correct when, eventually, all charges against her were dismissed.

The Polanski case kept them in touch, but it didn't bring them back together again. They stayed apart for a long while, although the ties that bind were never totally severed.

Nicholson kept himself busy on the social circuit, managing, among other conquests, an affair with Margaret Trudeau, the (then) estranged wife of Canadian Prime

Minister Pierre Trudeau. In her autobiographical volume *Consequences,* she wrote that Nicholson was "the first real rival to Pierre." She and Nicholson met during the summer of 1978, and as she recalled, their first evening together began with a "pleasurable night of flirting that ended in the back of the actor's chauffered car . . . I discovered just how much room there is in the back of a Daimler."

The affair didn't last long. Nicholson apparently had a bigger impact on her than she did on him, because he later confided to an interviewer, "While I went out with other women, I put my emotions in neutral, and my pride was never so wounded that I would never take [Anjelica] back. So when the reconciliation came, we never had to recriminate over who said what while we were apart . . . All the time she was away, I made it clear that I still wanted to see her. But I did it in a sort of negative way. There was none of that 'Hey, are you ready yet?' bull."

They returned to each other in the latter 1970s as equals. Both of them realized how important each was to the other. They made accommodations, came to understandings, changed. Nicholson conceded, "If you told me twenty years ago that some woman could go off and fuck one of my best friends, and I'd end up reading about in the newspapers, and that four years later I wouldn't even give a shit, I'd say, 'You're talking to the wrong guy here. That's not the way I am. I might want to be that guy, but I'm not.' Now I am."

During the time of the breakup and through the eventual reconciliation with Anjelica, Nicholson focused his creative energies on two movies, both of them westerns. In one, *The Missouri Breaks* (1976), he fulfilled a longtime desire: working with his idol, Marlon Brando. In the other, *Goin' South* (1979), he returned to the scene of one of his most bitter disappointments, directing, although this time he took on the added responsibility of directing himself.

The Missouri Breaks should have been a monster hit. It

should have been a great movie. It "coulda been a contender." The mere idea of acting icon Brando and his heir apparent, Nicholson, going at each other, toe to toe, on the silver screen stirred the blood of many a publicist. Their pairing was much written about and ballyhooed. Like *The Fortune* and *The Last Tycoon,* it seemed like a sure blockbuster. Never bet on a sure thing. Despite the presence of director Arthur *(Bonnie and Clyde* and *Little Big Man)* Penn, and hip novelist/screenwriter Thomas *(Rancho Deluxe)* McGuane, the film was a resounding, if peculiar, dud.

Nicholson was paid a whopping one million dollars to play horse thief Tom Logan. Brando, playing Robert E. Lee Clayton, the hired gun of the rich and powerful, cut an even better deal, earning five hundred thousand more than Nicholson and spending considerably less time in front of the cameras.

Nicholson didn't mind the disparity between the two salaries, nor did he mind the disproportionate workload. He was thrilled to be working with the mythic Brando. "I've never talked to an actor that Marlon wasn't one of their favorites," he said. He later admitted to author Douglas Brode, "I was up very early in the morning before I worked with Marlon Brando . . . It was like a first trip to New York."

The movie was an episodic, meandering tale, and the critics justifiably panned the production, yet gave the actors their due. Many critics, in fact, used the movie to rate the two stars against each other. Some had Brando the winner in the thespian shoot-out, while others called it a draw. Very few thought Nicholson outshone his idol, but then, Nicholson didn't wear a dress in the movie. Brando conceded that he had a distinct advantage in the contest. "Poor Jack Nicholson," he told a *Time* reporter. "He's right at the center, cranking the whole thing out, while I'm zipping around like a firefly."

* * *

After appearing in fifteen films between 1969 and 1976, Nicholson vanished from movie screens for nearly three years. He decided he needed a rest and he took two years off, spending a great deal of that time skiing in Aspen. It was also during this time that he and Anjelica found each other again.

When he finally decided to go back to work, he planned to direct (but not star in) a western called *Moontrap*. When that fell through, he settled on *Goin' South*, a rambunctious little goofball movie that he chose to both star in and direct. He was also deeply involved in the scripting of the movie, although he didn't receive a screen credit.

As a director, Nicholson has very definite strengths and weaknesses. His flaws? He readily admits, "I have a lousy narrative sense." What he's best at is working with actors, which one can see from the very start with his *Goin' South* casting choices. For instance, Mary Steenburgen was a total unknown, working as a waitress at New York's Magic Pan restaurant when she heard that Nicholson was auditioning actresses for a movie he was directing. According to writer Seth Cagin, "She wasn't even getting past the door to be considered when Nicholson saw her." He tested her and immediately knew she was perfect for the part of Julia Tate. He had to fight Paramount tooth and nail for the right to use her as his leading lady. He refused to back down and the studio finally relented. His discovery has become a highly regarded actress.

He had also tested Jessica Lange, who had been consigned to the actress junk heap after the *King Kong* remake debacle in 1976. Nicholson was impressed with her but didn't think she was right for Julia Tate. Not long after, when he made *The Postman Always Rings Twice*, he suggested to director Bob Rafelson that Lange might make an ideal Cora, and the deed was done: Nicholson had helped yet another actress become a star.

One need only witness how many other unknown actors he hired for *Goin' South* who later became major names to realize how good he was at picking talent. For instance,

John Belushi made his motion picture debut in the movie. Christopher Lloyd, who went on to fame as the scientist in *Back to the Future* and its sequels, had a role, and so did future comedy star/director Danny DeVito.

Nicholson did more than pick good actors. Steenburgen said that Nicholson was responsible for "teaching me how to put across the art of acting on film. Jack tells us how to eliminate the obvious and keep the simple. He directs by asking a helpful question or suggesting another way of approaching a scene."

Directing others was the easy part. "It's grueling work to direct and act at once," he conceded. When asked if he could pull it off, though, he said with a straight face, "It didn't hurt Molière, Shakespeare, or Pirandello."

For his own performance, Nicholson said, "I used everyone from Gabby Hayes to Spencer Tracy." He added, "It's not that I think of myself as a comic actor. It's that I think every character can be comical."

He saw the film itself as "light entertainment, but not sight gags. It's not *Cat Ballou*. We don't play the comedy. We play the reality of the events. Comedy," he insisted, "is born of reality."

For the most part, the critics didn't laugh. And the filmgoers simply didn't go. One can only guess at the reason, but a plausible explanation—which fits the failure of both *The Missouri Breaks* and *Goin' South*—is that Nicholson's fans are essentially an urban, sophisticated bunch. The western has long been out of favor with that audience (as it has for most audiences), and they simply weren't interested in seeing him in that milieu, no matter what he did or how he did it.

Nicholson saw the western differently. For him, it was the classic American genre. It was also a category in which he could fulfill his childhood fantasies. "All men love to play cowboy," he told an interviewer. "Actors are among the few men who can do it. They can shoot a gun, jump on a horse, or spin a pistol, and they're not considered schizophrenic." There was also an adult fantasy he wanted to fulfill: joining the ranks of Hollywood greats. "Cooper, Stewart, Tracy, Brando," he said wistfully. "They all made westerns."

Nicholson was understandably disappointed by the critical and commercial failure of *Goin' South*. He would not direct again for more than a decade. His next film, however, was almost as eagerly awaited in 1980 as *The Two Jakes* was in 1990. It was Stanley Kubrick's version of Stephen King's best-selling horror novel *The Shining*.

CHAPTER 15

"Just Because You're a Perfectionist Doesn't Mean You're Perfect"

"WITHIN THE NEXT six months, I will be something petrifying in between ten and one hundred million dreams," Nicholson said with glee after he finished shooting *The Shining*. The film was produced, directed, and cowritten by the famed director Stanley *(2001: A Space Odyssey)* Kubrick. Based on Stephen King's best-selling horror novel of the same name, it was a much-anticipated movie that everyone, both in and out of Hollywood, expected would be a tremendous critical and commercial hit when it was released in 1980.

For Nicholson, starring in his first horror film since Roger Corman's *The Raven* and *The Terror,* this was an upscale trip down memory lane. *The Shining* was to be the motion picture industry's first horror epic; what a triumph this would be for an actor who had spent all of two hours shooting his one scene in Corman's cheapie classic *The Little Shop of Horrors*.

Despite Nicholson's career stumbles during the latter half of the 1970s, there was no denying the pinnacle of prestige that came with starring in a Stanley Kubrick production. It was a pairing of star and director that was long in the making. Originally, Kubrick had contacted Nicholson in the very early 1970s about starring in a film about Napoleon. Nothing ever came of the project except the fueling of Nicholson's deep and abiding interest in the French leader's life. (He tried to make his own motion picture about Napoleon, but so far, nothing has come of that, either.) Now they were finally working together, the iconoclastic director who had fled Hollywood to make movies in England, and the equally iconoclastic star who was that rare Hollywood luminary crazy enough to play an ax murderer intent upon chopping up his wife and son.

Though Nicholson was willing to put his star status on the line to play such a thoroughly disreputable character, there were those who questioned whether he was an appropriate casting choice. That question was raised by none other than Stephen King himself, who wondered aloud in the press if the actor was capable of playing an "ordinary man."

Nicholson couldn't let it pass. "I have always played ordinary men," he pointedly responded. "I used to write, you know, so I understand the guy's [character Jack Torrance's] writer's block. I've been to school, so it's easy to figure out a teacher. [Torrance is a former teacher.] I'm Irish, so most of my family has had some sort of outburst related to alcoholism. [Torrance is an alcoholic.] I have an ex-wife I lived with for quite a while. I have a child, so I can understand fatherhood."

As it turned out, Nicholson was right. He gave a tour de force performance, but he gave it in a sadly mediocre and disappointing film. It wasn't the casting that was at fault, it was the script and the direction. The only reason to see this film is to watch Nicholson chew up the scenery. He is absolutely mesmerizing; you can't take your eyes off him.

There were critics who thought otherwise, who accused him of going way over the top, of giving a totally unrestrained performance. That, of course, was the whole joy of the film, making it both scary and funny at the same time. We had seen the devilish grin and the evil, flashing eyes before, but never had we seen them taken to such a theatrical, almost self-parodying, extreme. "Grand Guignol was that story's classification for me," Nicholson later explained. "And Grand Guignol should be fun. That's exactly how I felt about *The Shining.*" Yet even as he played his scenes, Nicholson kept worriedly exclaiming, "Jesus, Stanley, aren't I playing this too broad?"

Kubrick obviously didn't think so. After the movie was made, the director announced that Nicholson was "one of the truly great actors Hollywood has produced."

As always, Nicholson did more than merely act. Even with a director famous for exerting total control over his projects, Nicholson was intimately involved in making changes in the script. For instance, he added the moment to the scene where he chops partway through the bathroom door with his ax, sticks his head into the opening, and madly announces to his terrified wife, "Heeeeere's Johnny!" The phrase, famous in North America as the nightly introduction for the popular late night talk show host Johnny Carson, was completely unknown to Kubrick, who had been in self-exile in England since the early 1960s. He trusted that Nicholson knew what he was doing, and that scene remains one of the most memorable moments in the movie.

Nicholson was also responsible for the scene in the film that every author can relate to. It's the previously mentioned interruption of Torrance by his wife when he's trying to write. The actor explained the derivation of that scene to Ron Rosenbaum of the *New York Times:* "I was under the pressure of being a family man with a daughter, and one day I accepted a job to act in a movie in the daytime and I was writing a movie at night, and I'm back in my little corner and my beloved wife, Sandra, walked in on what was, unbeknownst to her, this *maniac*—and I told Stanley about it and we wrote it into the scene. I remember being at my desk and telling her: 'Even if you don't *hear* me typing, it doesn't mean I'm not *writing*. This *is* writing . . .' I remember that total animus. Well, I got a divorce."

Nicholson made his contributions, but it was still Kubrick's movie. The director's filmmaking style involved shooting an enormous number of takes of even the most mundane scenes, hoping that the camera would catch something extraordinary in one of them. The process was unlike anything Nicholson had ever experienced. Thirty, forty, fifty takes, and more, were not uncommon for scenes as minor as crossing a street without any dialogue.

Anjelica, who had accompanied Nicholson to London and had stayed with him during the shooting, said, "[Jack] would lurch into the house around ten P.M., exhausted. The one time we went out, we were an hour and a half late to meet Princess Margaret."

Nicholson didn't always see eye to eye with his vaunted director, particularly in Kubrick's work habits. "I'm a great off-stage grumbler," Nicholson admitted to a reporter from *Newsweek*. "I complained that [Kubrick] was the only director to light the sets with no stand-ins. We had to be there even to be lit. Just because you're a perfectionist doesn't mean you're perfect."

A great many critics concurred. So did audiences. *The Shining* did not meet their expectations.

At this point, it was five years since he'd had a hit with *Cuckoo's Nest*. Soon, however, he had something far more important to worry about. Anjelica was in a traffic accident. In a collision with another vehicle, she went head-first through the windshield of her car and suffered a badly broken nose. She spent six hours under a plastic surgeon's knife, recuperating from her ordeal at Nicholson's house.

It was at about this time that Nicholson proclaimed, "I certainly would say [Anjelica's] the love of my life . . . We've strived for a straightforward, honest, yet mature relationship . . . She has to do the hardest work in that area, because I'm the one who is so easily gossiped about . . . I live with Anjelica," he continued, "and there are other women in my life who are simply friends of mine. Most of the credit for our wonderfully successful relationship has to do with her flexibility."

He would severely test that flexibility in the years ahead.

CHAPTER 16

"Somebody Else Might Have Said I Was a Pervert"

SEX. IT WAS the reason Nicholson decided to make *The Postman Always Rings Twice* (1981). "I'm drawn to the sensual area of acting, and since that's the central thrust of this story, I felt it was ideal for me," he told an interviewer.

Postman is about more than just sex. It's also about murder, betrayal, and the intensity of emotion. Nicholson himself had been rather intense to make the film, having tried to get it on the screen in the early 1970s with his then current girlfriend, Michelle Phillips. The project fell through when the studio insisted that Raquel Welch play the female lead. At that point, Nicholson immediately dropped out.

Several years later, when pal Bob Rafelson got involved with the project, Nicholson took a new interest. Everything finally began falling into place.

David Mamet, the Pulitzer prizewinning playwright, adapted the screenplay from the hard-boiled novel by James M. Cain. Cain's story had been made into a hit movie before, with Lana Turner and John Garfield, but the new version was darker, meaner, and very, very *hot*.

The question in the minds of many was, why remake a movie that was already considered a classic? Nicholson had his reasons. "I have rarely spoken to anyone who didn't love the 1945 Lana Turner movie," he conceded. "For all of us, it was a favorite melodrama. And John

Garfield was one of my favorite actors. I wouldn't want to remake *Body and Soul* or something else where Garfield was on his best turf. The only reason why I redid *Postman* is that nobody has ever filmed the original material before . . . No one has actually filmed the book.''

On another occasion he further explained, ''This is a particular kind of love story—the kind of sudden, illicit, lustful, pathological story that Hollywood couldn't concern itself with at a certain point . . . It's like you know a good song when you hear one. And that's what I heard in *Postman*, something in which to play on my idiosyncrasies as an actor.''

Nicholson saw his character of Frank Chambers in an entirely different light than he had been shown in the original version of the film. ''Whereas that character has been played very charmingly,'' he said, ''the fact of the matter is, he's a sadist who solved every problem he ever had in his life with violence . . . I don't particularly want a guy who murders a man and then fucks his wife on top of her husband's body to be all *that* charming.''

There was never any doubt as to who was going to play Frank Chambers. Cora, from the very beginning, had been the difficult casting decision. ''It's the role most every actress in Hollywood wanted to play,'' Nicholson once said. Finding the right chemistry, however, proved to be elusive. At one point, rumor has it, Meryl Streep was approached for the part. She supposedly said she would only do full frontal nudity if Nicholson did. Nicholson referred to that bit of scuttlebutt as ''cute.'' In fact, none of the actors appeared naked (frontal or otherwise) in the final version of the film except for a brief partial shot of Nicholson's rear end.

The role of Cora ultimately went to a surprise choice, Jessica Lange, whom Nicholson had tested for *Goin' South*. ''She was the great gift,'' Nicholson said of Lange after shooting *Postman*. ''. . . She's sexy, and she makes me sexy, too, which takes a lot of doing. It's like the

Astaire concept, where Ginger Rogers gave Astaire a certain kind of appeal that none of his other partners could.''

The sexiness the two brought to the screen was electric. Their torrid lovemaking scenes were at once shockingly erotic and passionately violent. Despite almost uniformly bad reviews when the movie opened, those sex scenes were the talk of rank-and-file filmgoers everywhere.

''Doing it [the sex scenes] on-screen has to be real, like drinking a cup of coffee,'' Nicholson said. In a quest for that reality, Nicholson said, ''I wanted to have a full stinger, because they'd never seen that in movies. I just knew this odd image would be a stunner. Well, I went upstairs and worked on it for forty-five minutes, but I couldn't get anything going because I knew everyone was waiting down there to see this thing. Somebody else might have said I was a pervert, but in my terms, this would've been extremely artful.''

Despite Nicholson's opinion that *Postman* was ''a stunner, lustful and hot,'' the movie did not get the good word of mouth needed to make a hit after a majority of the important critics had dismissed it. Once again, though, Nicholson was singled out for praise in another losing cause. Or at least it appeared to be a losing cause. It turned out that *Postman* became a major hit virtually everywhere in the world except North America. The movie actually outgrossed one of Nicholson's biggest hits, *Chinatown,* in almost all of the overseas markets.

Why did it fail in the United States? ''I think the American audience just wasn't ready to get hot in the theater,'' said Nicholson.

It seemed as if Nicholson was intent upon making a movie in every genre. He had appeared in at least one musical, detective story, western, contemporary drama, service comedy, horror film, and comedy since becoming a star. But he hadn't as yet appeared in an action film. *The Border* (1981) took care of that oversight.

''I wanted to do an action movie before I was really too

old to do it,'' he told an interviewer. After *The Border* was made, he admitted, ''It's one of the most physically demanding things I've ever done, because of the repetition. It doesn't mean anything to jump off a car, but to jump off a car twenty times . . .''

Just as *The Missouri Breaks* was nothing like your usual horse opera, and *The Shining* was hardly a typical horror film, *The Border* was a very different sort of action movie. Well, at least it tried to be.

Viewed as an ambitious failure, *The Border* received mostly poor reviews. Again, he had starred in a film that did not meet expectations at the box office. As always, though, Nicholson received his fair share of good notices for work that transcended the script.

Unfortunately, after six years of disappointing ticket sales and mixed reviews, it appeared as if moviegoers were no longer interested in him, whether he was good or bad. The critics had been carping for years about Nicholson's film choices; now he was paying the piper. Nonetheless, he took it philosophically. ''I always had this horrible feeling I was being overly praised, and I knew, sooner or later, it would come back at me,'' he said. ''Despite all the criticism,'' he added, ''the real challenge is to stay creatively alive.''

That's what he did.

Though he was described as the ''Actor of the 1970s'' during the first half of that decade, his star had fallen very far indeed. No one expected him to be the ''Actor of the 1980s,'' but in 1981, the same year he made *The Postman Always Rings Twice* and *The Border,* he also made *Reds,* and that was the first step in his drive to reclaim his stature as Hollywood's most unpredictable, most versatile, and most talented actor. Or, as he impishly prefers to be called, ''a megasuperstar.''

CHAPTER 17

The Terms of Success

IF NICHOLSON HADN'T already established a willingness to take roles that other stars would have avoided, his appearance in modest supporting parts in *Reds* (1981) and *Terms of Endearment* (1983) would have certainly signaled his superstar demise. After six years of critical and/ or commercial duds, many might have suspected that he was no longer capable of carrying a major motion picture, and had no other choice but to play supporting roles. Nicholson, on the other hand, could convincingly claim that he simply liked these particular small roles and wanted to play them. His past history made such statements utterly believable.

"You know," he pointed out, "*Easy Rider* was the part that made the public sort of aware of me, and that's only twenty-something minutes on the screen. I've always wanted to protect my right as an actor to play a short part without everyone thinking my career is over. And so I've always intermittently done them [e.g., *Tommy* and *The Last Tycoon*]. I mean, they come around every once in a while anyway, and when I see a good one and I've got the space, I'll probably do it . . ."

The space was there when his friend Warren Beatty gave him a call and asked him to play the small but important role of writer Eugene O'Neill in his directorial debut, *Reds*. "[Beatty] asked me to play it for very good superstructural cinematic reasons," said Nicholson. Simply put, these two men, whom the public knew to be friends, who had gone girl-chasing together, and who had shared at least one lover

(Michelle Phillips), made perfect casting sense as romantic rivals. In fact, it was typecasting.

There were undoubtedly several reasons why Nicholson took the part. Loyalty was one of them; Nicholson will do most anything for a friend. Another reason was his continuing desire to stretch himself; he said he "hadn't done much biographical acting," and this role gave him that opportunity. And then there was the obvious reason: "That was one of the most cleanly written parts I've ever played," he told an interviewer. "I figured, if I'm not any good in this, I ought to be shot."

On the surface, one had to wonder if being shot wouldn't be preferable to appearing in a massively budgeted opus (estimated at over $35 million) that was being made by a first-time director, and that chose American communists (now, there's a topic the U.S. public will rush out to see) as its subject matter. Warren Beatty the producer had a lot of confidence in Warren Beatty the novice director, who, in turn, had high hopes for Warren Beatty's screenplay, while hoping that Warren Beatty the actor had the drawing power to keep *Reds* from becoming a humiliating fiasco.

As it turned out, all four Warren Beattys proved their mettle in this intelligent and finely produced saga of writer John Reed, the author of *Ten Days That Shook the World* (a book about the 1917 Russian Revolution). Wisely, Beatty didn't dwell overmuch on the politics. Instead, he showed his audience a tug of war between the grand romance shared by Reed and Louise Bryant (Diane Keaton), and Reed's ultimate disillusionment with his most cherished idealistic beliefs, set against the action-filled backdrop of battle and revolution.

Nicholson's role in all this Sturm und Drang came early in the proceedings. Louise Bryant, a liberated woman, is torn between her love of the romantic dreamer, Reed, with whom she is already involved, and of the cynical realist, O'Neill, who has become enamored of her. The triangle deepens by virtue of the fact that Reed and O'Neill are good friends.

Life suddenly mirrored art. Nicholson conceded that at one point during the making of the movie, he began having very deep feelings for Diane Keaton (who, at that time, was also Beatty's lover). "There is something actorish about thinking, 'My God, I've got a real crush, and holy fuck, this is my best friend and his girlfriend,' " Nicholson said. "But that's also what the movie was about," he continued. "My character was attracted to Keaton's character. And I'm focused on my job all the time."

He was so focused, in fact, that in a scene in which he gives her a love poem, he told an interviewer, "I wrote a real poem that was extremely revealing." Nicholson's poem was "in that envelope when I gave it to her on camera. It's the kind of thing no one else sees, but you know it's there. And believe me, I did not misplace that prop," he added.

In the end, nothing ever happened between Nicholson and Keaton. "I'm not an asshole," he said.

Nicholson's deep involvement in the role of Eugene O'Neill proved to be a tonic for his ailing career. When the movie opened to generally good reviews, he was singled out for special praise. For instance, *Newsweek's* David Ansen wrote, "Nicholson, as the cynical, boozing O'Neill, plays the devil's advocate to the romantic revolutionists—and almost steals the picture. He has three razor-sharp scenes with Keaton in which hostility and lust mingle with caustic menace. It's his best work in years."

The best review he received wasn't in a newspaper or a magazine. Oona O'Neill Chaplin, the estranged daughter of the playwright, wrote to Nicholson, who said of the letter's content, "It's the greatest compliment I ever got. She says something like, 'After a lifetime of acquired indifference, the inevitable finally happened. Thanks to you, dear Jack, I fell in love with my father.' "

Having taken the role, in part, out of loyalty to Beatty (whom he called "Master B."), he had no desire to upstage him. At every opportunity, Nicholson deferred to his friend and director. "I love being praised," he said, "but after all, my efforts are so minimal compared to his [Beatty's] . . . No one's taken on a job of that magnitude, with so many difficult points in it. The fact that he actually pulled it off is a great achievement. I just played another part in a movie where the conditions for me were ideal—beautifully written part, great actress to work with, a director very sympathetic to the needs of an actor in order to be able to function. In terms of justice, I hope all praise would fall to him, because I know the effort it's been.''

Nonetheless, his own efforts were rewarded with his second Best Supporting Actor Academy Award nomination, and his sixth Oscar nomination overall. He didn't win, but at least his reputation as an actor of skill and merit had been rerecognized by his peers.

Not long after his triumph in *Reds,* Nicholson became seriously interested in another biographical role, this one in a film called *Ernest and Mary,* in which he would have played the role of Ernest Hemingway. It might have made an interesting companion piece to his portrayal of O'Neill, but even though the screenplay was written with Nicholson in mind, the movie was never made.

Instead of leaping into another role, he decided to take some time off again. This time, as well as skiing, he saw his daughter's high school graduation in Hawaii and enjoyed himself at Wimbledon. ''I'd been to England a couple of years before but I was working every day [on *The Shining*] and so I didn't get a chance to see the tennis,'' he explained. ''And I also spent the summer in the south of France relaxing, then came home and went skiing in Colorado.''

Outside of filming, Nicholson loves to ski when he's on vacation. ''I wake up every morning tired when I'm working,'' he said. ''I've been tired so long it's a joke. That's why I love skiing. I wake up in the morning and I'm tired. And I get up. Then I ski all day and for some reason I'm not tired. The next morning I'm tired again but I know I'm going skiing and that's what gets me through. I make the effort even though I'm tired. Once I sit down in the chair-lift to the top of the mountain, everything's okay again.''

Nearly two years passed before he reappeared on the big screen, during which time Anjelica moved out of his house. But not out of his life. ''I had a good life living with Jack,'' she told Aljean Harmetz, ''but it was necessary to remove myself from the entourage a career like his engenders. I had never lived alone. I didn't even know what color I liked my coffee in the morning.'' She didn't move far, getting a house very close to his. The romance was still on, only now they had their own separate lives. In addition, Anjelica had decided to pursue an acting career with a more single-minded energy, and she didn't want to be lost in Jack's shadow.

Just the same, in the early 1980s he wasn't casting a very long shadow. *Reds* had been a personal success, but the movie was not a big enough hit to immediately earn back its colossal expense. More to the point, he had been off the screen for so long that when he finally reappeared in another supporting role in the 1983 film *Terms of Endearment,* his performance was considered by many to be a comeback.

Comeback or not, his portrayal of ex-astronaut Garrett Breedlove was a sharp departure from his previous roles. It was such a success that many interviewers felt compelled to ask him about the long string of failures that had preceded it. Except Nicholson didn't see it that way. He insisted that the years after *Cuckoo's Nest* until *Terms* were ''extremely productive, creatively adventurous, aesthetically rewarding, exciting, and vital. I'm very proud of that body of work, even though it's consistently been written about in a light-that-failed metaphor.''

He neglected to mention that none of the films during that stretch of time were major commercial hits. In order to have a wide choice of roles in Hollywood, a certain percentage of one's movies have to make a profit. A sizable profit is recommended.

He once commented that he had been "angry" in the 1970s and, as a consequence, had done a lot of "murder films." When he was ready to return to the screen, he said, "I decided to come back playing a guy as lovable as you can possibly get." Another way of putting it is that he wanted to change his image.

Nicholson read the script of *Terms of Endearment* and realized that he could really add something to the movie. He told an interviewer that he imagined "quite a few other actors" could play Garrett Breedlove, "but I knew it wouldn't have as good an effect on this movie if someone else played it." It had to be him. Besides, there were elements in Breedlove's character that very definitely appealed to him. For one thing, "This part is closer to the way I feel about life, which is 'Let the good times roll.' "

When the film was announced, industry pundits thought that the movie would be a major dud. Who, they wondered, would want to see a story about a middle-aged mother (Shirley MacLaine) who has a daughter (Debra Winger) dying of cancer? Nicholson knew better. He took the role "principally because I thought they would definitely hit the bull's-eye, because it *wasn't* about mechanized robots or puppets or monsters or special effects . . . They took a big central theme that was about human beings, and that's what I felt would make it successful . . . because there weren't any others around."

He had finally picked a winner. The critics loved the film, and audiences laughed and cried and recommended it to their friends. It was a substantial hit.

So was Nicholson. Critics loved the fact that he allowed himself to look decidedly middle-aged. "Normally, I lose weight for a movie," Nicholson explained. "This time, they asked me not to, and I gave them the baby elephant pregnant look."

Rewarded for his wonderfully natural performance with yet another Oscar nomination, Nicholson was flamboyantly honest, saying, "I think you've got to have nutty goals in life. I'd like to win more Oscars than Walt Disney, and I'd like to win them in every category. And I've been after this category [Best Supporting Actor] for a while.''

Nicholson won. Look out, Walt (wherever you are).

Nicholson hasn't always confined his performances to the big screen. A monumentally committed basketball fan with a special devotion to the Los Angeles Lakers, the actor has been known to rearrange his shooting schedules and travel plans in order to either watch, listen to, or personally attend a game. And sometimes he doesn't just watch.

At one point during the 1984 NBA play-offs between the legendary Boston Celtics and his beloved Lakers, Nicholson got so wrapped up in the series that he began publicly taunting the Celtic fans—*in the Boston Garden*. From the safety of his private box overlooking the court, he made the ''choke'' sign (indicating that the Celtics couldn't stand the pressure and would lose) by holding his throat with his hand. He had done that before, and many Celtic fans were prepared for him, bringing signs to the old arena that read ''Jack, Choke on Coke,'' ''Hit the Road, Jack,'' and ''Sorry Jack, under the Terms, This One's Over the Cuckoo's Nest.'' As the game neared its end, with the Celtics about to win, Nicholson drove the crowd to a frenzy by reportedly dropping his trousers and ''mooning'' the entire sold-out crowd at the Boston Garden. After the game, he had to leave his private box under police protection.

Nicholson stayed zipped ever since, but he's been no less a vociferous fan. For the most part, though, basketball players from other teams don't mind Jack's antics. They do resent celebrity fans who only come out to games in order to be seen on TV or otherwise get publicity, but they recognize that Nicholson is a genuine fan who really loves basketball; he comes whether his team is playing in L.A. or in less media-oriented cities like Cleveland and Seattle. Even the Celtics don't mind him. At least not anymore.

* * *

Nicholson is competitive in yet another court: of the legal variety. If he thinks he's been wronged, he'll sue—no matter how small-seeming the claim. For instance, he had a pet dog, a Lhasa apso, that was attacked by another dog near the actor's Aspen, Colorado hideaway. His dog was badly bitten on the stomach and back by a German shepherd, and Nicholson went to court, filing for damages against the attacking dog's owner, a local dentist. The dentist got drilled when the judge found in Nicholson's favor, awarding the actor $769.20 for veterinarian bills, while also ruling that the dentist had to fence his dog in and send the offending pooch to obedience school.

Nicholson goes after big fish as well as big dogs. He sued media baron Rupert Murdoch's famous London tabloid, the *Sun,* for libel. The newspaper interviewed the actor in early 1984 and included in its copy that the actor had had "a string of drug busts in America." It wasn't so. Nicholson might have been incredibly open and honest about his drug use, but he had never been arrested for doing dope.

The case did not come to trial, as the *Sun* settled out of court for what Nicholson's London attorney, Desmond Browne, referred to as "substantial" damages. In addition, the newspaper offered Nicholson an unqualified apology for their error.

He may be litigious, but when he sues, he sues to win. And he usually does.

You'll see Nicholson in movies, women's bedrooms, basketball arenas, and court, but the one place you'll never see him is on a television talk show. He simply will not appear on TV to promote either his films or himself. He never has, and vows that he never will.

Way back during his struggling years, when he said he didn't do TV, Nicholson simply meant he wouldn't act in the medium. Once he hit it big and was being offered the opportunity to simply appear on various shows as himself, Nicholson decided that it would be a huge mistake for him to do it. He reasoned that going on TV talk shows broke down the mystery between the audience and the actor. If people knew him as a person from these shows, it would make it that much harder for him to create new characters on-screen that the audience would accept as "him."

Although most actors promote their movies by hitting the talk-show circuit, Nicholson has proven that he need not follow the rules in order to be a star. Of course, he rarely follows the rules, and that has been the key element of his success throughout his long and remarkable career—a career that was just about to head into overdrive.

CHAPTER 18

Nicholson's Honor

NICHOLSON, WHO WORKED with the likes of Bob Rafelson, Mike Nichols, Roman Polanski, and Stanley Kubrick, once said, "I try to work with the best director available. Once you've got your material, the director is the guy who puts it into action. I think the reason for the success I've had is I got great taste in directors." The same reason has been given for the great screen success of Humphrey Bogart (with whom Nicholson has often been compared). He worked with many of the great directors of his day, most notably John Huston, who directed Bogie in six of his best-remembered films. It was time for the new Bogie to work with the old Bogie's best director. In doing so, Nicholson was inspired to one of his most effective performances in *Prizzi's Honor* (1985) by the last living directorial titan of the Hollywood era, John Huston.

The director was insistent upon making this bleak, black, infinitely cynical comedy. First, however, he had to assemble his cast. And without a big-name star, the movie would likely never have been funded. Anjelica signed on first, getting her role not through nepotism, but because of John Foreman, the producer. Foreman had produced the poorly received *The Ice Pirates* (1984), in which Anjelica had had a small part, and he strongly suggested her for the pivotal role of Maerose Prizzi, the manipulative character who drives the plot. The director needed little convincing. "I instantly agreed," he said.

Getting Anjelica didn't automatically mean getting Jack.

Kathleen Turner was the next to sign up, and she was the one who forced Nicholson's hand. According to Lawrence Grobel's *The Hustons,* she called Nicholson up to tell him that she had turned down another film role to play Irene (the California hit woman who marries into the Brooklyn mob) and she felt she had a right to know whether or not he was going to commit to the production.

Turner apparently pushed him off the fence, and he landed feet first into the role of Charley Partanna (the Brooklyn hit man loved by Maerose but who marries Irene). Turner was thrilled to be working with him. She had made her own commitment to the film in the hope of working with both Huston and Nicholson. And her dream had come true. As for Nicholson, she said, "It's great to work with an actor and never worry about the 'nets.' If I get an idea in the middle of a scene, I can go all the way with it. All I have to do is act; he can follow, he can lead—anything!"

Curiously, Nicholson's original reluctance to take the part can be traced to a very simple reason: "I honestly didn't understand it [the story] at the beginning," he said. "I didn't have any grasp of the character. I saw it like a humorless person would. I read it as a very straight sort of story, and didn't really get it."

Nicholson was torn. "I told John, 'I've been wanting to work with you,' but I don't know if you want me in a picture I don't understand."

In due time, Huston took him aside and in a stage whisper said, "It's a comedy, Jack."

Ultimately Nicholson agreed to star in the film largely because of his desire to work with Huston: "I think he's the current king of the world," he declared. "People, truck drivers, they recognize me, but for him, they open the door."

Once he agreed to be in the picture, Nicholson began to create his character. It started with Huston saying, "It seems to me, Jack, everything you've done is informed by intelligence. And you can't have that with this film. It's got to be dumb, very dumb." Curiously, Nicholson's Charley Partanna is not "very dumb." Rather, he is relatively uneducated and unsophisticated. He isn't so much dumb as he is simple. Nicholson well understood the difficulty of his role. "What I wanted to do," he explained to an interviewer, "was to be able to play that farcical comic character and still have the audience believe that if there's a problem, he takes care of it very clean, because he's the best. And that's what the movie ultimately says."

Once the character was clarified in his mind, the next thing Nicholson had to do was bring him physically to life. He did that by putting on thirty pounds. "I didn't have to gain weight, but I did anyway because I ingested the part," he explained. "I wanted the guy to be a heavy in that sense."

After the weight gain came the tissues stuffed into his mouth. Unlike Marlon Brando in *The Godfather,* who stuffed cotton in his cheeks, Nicholson crammed pieces of tissue behind his upper lip, "to immobilize that part of my face," making it stiff and unmoving like so many of the older Italian men he had observed in Brooklyn bars while doing his research for the role.

Then came those flat, cold, brutishly conniving eyes. Nicholson said he took them "from the eyes of my dog when he killed another dog."

The crowning achievement of his characterization, what lifted the killer to comic proportions, was the accent: It was a broad Italian Brooklynese that had audiences laughing as soon as he opened his mouth. Not as overtly comical as Chico Marx's intentionally bad broken English, Nicholson's accent was a nostalgic re-creation of a 1940s Old World idiom, making it both realistic and anachronistic at the same time.

Prizzi's Honor was very much a family affair. Huston was directing his daughter, who was acting with her lover, who, in turn, considered Huston a father figure. As Nicholson once said of John Huston: "He's one of those people in life whose approval I seek."

Both John Huston and Jack Nicholson wanted Anjelica to shine in *Prizzi*. Quite by accident, on the first day of shooting, Anjelica caught a visual image that put her mind at ease about the making of this movie. "I looked up to see my father perfectly framed in one of the trellises outside the ballroom set and Jack perfectly framed in another, and it was like a gift," she told Aljean Harmetz. "I knew my father would do his best to make me look good, and Jack wouldn't belittle me."

Despite the fact that Jack and Anjelica had been together by that time for twelve years ("longer than any of my five marriages lasted," said John Huston), they didn't stay at the same hotel during the making of *Prizzi*. According to Anjelica, Nicholson was taking his character home with him, and as she put it, he "had a little too much of the hit man in him." In addition to his apparent belligerence, he also maintained his best Brooklyn underworld accent whether on or off camera, a practice that the crew found vastly entertaining.

Nicholson became so involved in the project that he even went so far as to suggest an advertising slogan for the film, "Killers: You Always Hurt the One You Love." Regrettably, they didn't use it.

The $15 million movie was made exceptionally fast. "I had more one-takes in this picture than I have had since I worked with Roger Corman," Nicholson commented wryly. When he saw the finished product, he didn't mince words: "I think it's one of the best things I've done."

The critics agreed. At least most of them did. *Time* magazine's Richard Schickel called it "one of his boldest performances." *Newsweek*'s David Ansen said Nicholson's work was "a masterful turn." The influential Pauline Kael of *The New Yorker* wrote, "Nicholson doesn't overdo his blurred expressions or his uncomprehending stare; he's a witty actor who keeps you eager for what he'll do next.''

Despite the hype that one might expect from the film's producer, John Foreman probably best expressed what was so impressive about Nicholson's performance. He told a reporter for *People* magazine that playing Partanna ''really put Jack through the wringer. It forced him to give up everything the public has loved about him—his smile, his charm, his wit, his way of letting you in on the character's naughty secrets. It took great courage to do what Jack did.''

Nicholson was recognized for his achievement by the New York Film Critics, who gave him his record-breaking fifth Best Actor award.

He wasn't the only one being praised for his work in the film. Even though *Prizzi's Honor* only did modest box office, it did wonderfully well with Academy members. It racked up eight Oscar nominations, including Best Actor for Nicholson (his eighth), Best Supporting Actress for Anjelica, Best Director, and Best Picture. Unfortunately, only one of them bore fruit, but it was sweet fruit, indeed . . .

Anjelica won the Best Supporting Actress Academy Award, setting a record for three generations of Oscar winners in one family. Walter Huston, directed by John, had won a Best Supporting Actor Oscar for *The Treasure of the Sierra Madre* in 1948, and John himself had won the Best Director Oscar for the same film. Now John had directed both his father and his daughter to Academy Award-winning performances.

Nicholson was ecstatic with Anjelica's victory. With a cast on his left elbow due to a skiing accident, he still managed to wildly applaud using one hand and a leg. That the voters overlooked him in favor of William Hurt (for *Kiss of the Spider Woman*) didn't appear to bother him at all. After Anjelica won, he told a reporter, ''That's all we wanted out of the night. Just wanted one for Toots.''

Later he told Janet Maslin, ''I've got big hopes that this will give her [Anjelica] an opportunity to be more expansive. I didn't do anything to make her this good, but I was proud to be around her when it happened.''

CHAPTER 19

As Versatile as Hell

WHY WOULD NICHOLSON, one of Hollywood's most sought-after actors, jump into a troubled project at the last minute, accept second billing, and take a role for which he was clearly miscast? Two reasons: loyalty and adventure. The loyalty was to director Mike Nichols, who had previously directed the actor in *Carnal Knowledge* and *The Fortune*. The adventure was to work with Hollywood's most talented actress, Meryl Streep. That the movie was an adaptation of Nora Ephron's highly publicized best-selling novel *Heartburn* was of little matter in the decision. As it turned out, the movie was of little matter, as well.

Ephron's thinly veiled autobiographical novel was based on her marriage to, and subsequent divorce from, famed *Washington Post* reporter and author Carl Bernstein (who had been previously portrayed by Dustin Hoffman in *All the President's Men*). The novel was a biting, satiric stab at the heart. The 1986 movie was not.

It could have been a hard-hitting film about the fragile bonds that hold people together—and sometimes break them apart. Instead, the first half of the movie was a pleasant if innocuous romantic/domestic comedy. Then, suddenly, the second half took a sharp turn into a poorly written, badly motivated domestic tragedy.

What doomed the movie to mediocrity was a lawsuit instituted by Carl Bernstein. He knew that if *Heartburn* was faithfully adapted into a movie, he would become a synonym for villainy to women everywhere. A best-selling book might reach as many as a million people, but a movie (and the reality that it represents) would be seen by tens of millions in theaters, on TV, on videocassettes; it would haunt him on late night movie shows for the rest of his life. So he fought the movie after ignoring the publication of the book.

Rather than see the project mired in endless legal hassles, Ephron settled out of court, giving in to many of Bernstein's demands. As a result, the script was substantially watered down. Another result was that actor Mandy Patinkin, originally hired to play Streep's husband, Mark, quit the production after shooting had begun.

Director Nichols, in need of a quality actor in a hurry, was delighted when Nicholson agreed to stand in as Streep's husband two weeks into the shoot. Loyalty, however, is one thing. Nicholson was too big a star to lend his name and credibility to the project *purely* as a favor: He was reportedly paid $4 million.

There were two problems with casting Nicholson as Mark. To begin with, he was too old for the part. But that's a minor point. More important, he brought such a winning style to the role that Mark became a genuinely lovable guy. Sure, he cheated on his wife, but the film never explained his motives. As far as the audience was concerned, Mark might have had perfectly defensible reasons; he certainly didn't seem like a heel or a cad. Without presenting reasons for his cheating, the movie lost its focus.

Still, it was worth the price of admission just to see Nicholson and Streep together on the screen—especially when they launched into a hilarious rendition of "baby" songs (Her character had just announced her first pregnancy) while eating a pizza. The topper was Nicholson's comically intense singing of the "Soliloquy" from *Carousel* (aka "My Boy, Bill").

A great scene does not a movie make. The critics killed *Heartburn*, and audiences buried it in indifference. Saddled with a meandering, pointless script, the two stars couldn't fully show their stuff. They would get their chance again the following year in *Ironweed*, and prove—Oscar or no Oscar—that they are, as *People* magazine put it, "two of the greatest actors on the planet."

1987 was a spectacular year for Nicholson. He appeared in three films, playing three wildly different types of characters, and all to enormous critical acclaim. His awesomely outrageous devil in *The Witches of Eastwick*, followed by an unbilled, scene-stealing stint as an anchorman in the hit *Broadcast News*, and topped off by his poignant, shattering performance as Francis Phelan in *Ironweed*, were a body of work that displayed Nicholson at the very top of his form.

The Witches of Eastwick was the first of his three films released in 1987. Loosely based on a John Updike novel of the same name, the movie tells the story of three beautiful young women in a small New England town who, through their wishful reveries, conjure up the devil to both seduce them and, ultimately, liberate them.

The Witches of Eastwick was that seemingly happy accident where an actor and a role were destined for each other. Just as George Burns was perfectly cast as God, Jack Nicholson was born to play the devil. Initially, however, the film's director, George Miller, didn't see Nicholson for the part of Darryl Van Horne; Miller wanted to cast against type, going for a more wholesome-looking character. Nonetheless, the director kept his options open and eventually "realized he [Nicholson] is like a two-hundred-year-old child; very wise in many ways, even beyond his years, but with a certain innocence and naïveté we expect from someone younger. The moment I saw that, I knew he was the only actor to bring a humanity to the role, to pull the devil out of stereotype."

Once Nicholson had agreed to play Van Horne, casting the three witches quickly fell into place. Cher, Michelle Pfeiffer, and Susan Sarandon were the three beauties bedded and bedeviled by Nicholson in this sexy parable about the war between the genders. Interestingly, Anjelica Huston went after Cher's role, making her test just a short while after winning her Best Supporting Actress Oscar for *Prizzi's Honor*. Admittedly nervous, she thought her reading was poor, and evidently she was right. She was passed over for the part.

Both Cher and Michelle Pfeiffer went after their roles in *Witches* because of their strong desire to work with Nicholson—and they were glad they did, despite the often troubled production. "We were all Jack's girls," said Cher, "and we would always go to him when we couldn't take any more. He would listen to us, lovingly, and then go fight our fights for us. As a male superstar, he could stand up to the Hollywood establishment in a way we couldn't, and he never once failed to take our part."

Nicholson was not only a spokesman for the three actresses, he was also their guru. Just as the "witches" relied on Van Horne, so did they rely on Jack. For instance, Cher recalled that she was "getting ready to do the buffet scene on the lawn, and for some reason I got an anxiety attack. I could hardly move. I was terrified. I went to Jack's trailer and told him something was wrong. And he put his arm around me and said, 'Look, it's free-floating anxiety, nerves. You're all right. We don't have to go out there and work. Nobody's gonna do this scene until we're ready.' And the minute he said that, I started to feel really good. That day, he was like a miracle."

The real miracle, though, was that the movie turned out as well as it did, considering that the producers, Neil Canton, Peter Guber, and Jon Peters, could not make up their minds as to what kind of picture they were making. The script seemed to change almost every day. At one point the movie was going to be a sex romp. At another point, it was going to be built largely around special effects. One interpretation of the script had Van Horne toned down, and another had him extravagantly extroverted. The conflicts over story, style, and tone led George Miller to actually shoot each scene eight different ways, finally settling on a combination of comedy and special effects, but using Nicholson's most over-the-top scenes, finding that "the broader takes were the ones that played best."

They sure did.

The movie was a smash hit, earning generally mixed to good reviews and, better still, upwards of $125 million at the box office. All of the witches gave strong, sensual performances, particularly Susan Sarandon. It was Nicholson, though, who was thoroughly riveting. Pauline Kael said, "Jack Nicholson entertains himself in *Witches,* and damned if he doesn't entertain us, too." But it was *New York Daily News* film critic Kathleen Carroll who hit the mark when she wrote: "No one really has a chance as long as Jack Nicholson, in a samurai hairdo and brocade lounging robe, is chewing up the scenery as Van Horne. He hams it up with a gleeful vengeance."

In *Ironweed,* released just before the end of 1987 in order to qualify for Oscar consideration, Nicholson gave a performance that was diametrically opposed in both tone and style to his scene-stomping portrayal in *Witches.* So thoroughly immersed was he in his character of a homeless alcoholic in Albany, New York, during 1938 that he hardly looked or even sounded like himself. His restrained, subtle, detailed playing of a man haunted by his past mistakes was arguably the greatest performance of his career.

He was joined in the cast by Meryl Streep, who played his vagabond girlfriend, Helen. After the disappointing *Heartburn,* they found a project in *Ironweed* that allowed their talents to grow and flourish. "Helen is one of Meryl's greatest transformations," Nicholson proudly said of his costar. And Meryl joked that "Jack turned fifty on this project, most of the time he looked seventy . . . but what he's done is tremendous."

Their professional admiration for each other was deep and unmistakable. There were also rumors that Nicholson and Streep admired each other rather personally. "Jack is an extraordinary being," she told an interviewer. "He's one of the few people that, when I'm with him, I feel surrounded by about eighty people. Ambushed!'' Whether or not they actually had a love affair, there was no question about the love she had for him as an artist. ''I think he's a master,'' she explained. ''He's got a voracious appetite for the work and the quality of the work. He's never satisfied, he's always churning. Energy! Fire in the belly! . . . It's wild. There's nobody out there that far in the movies. Nobody!''

Ironweed was a Pulitzer prizewinning novel by William Kennedy, and the author adapted his own work for the screen. Hector Babenco, who had previously directed the award-winning *Kiss of the Spider Woman* (1985), was named to direct the film. This was yet another case of Nicholson picking his films largely on the basis of the quality of the director's work, because he had read the book and had not been terribly impressed with it.

While Nicholson remained uncommitted to the prestigious project, other actors pursued it, among them Gene Hackman, Jason Robards, and Sam Shepard. But according to William Kennedy, ''Nicholson had that toughness, that Irishness'' that the role ultimately called for.

The success of *Prizzi's Honor* and subsequent Oscar nomination had upped Nicholson's price per picture. He agreed to star in *Ironweed* for $5 million. The film's budget was $27 million, and at that price tag, *Ironweed* could not afford merely to be an art house hit. That's why the movie's producer, Keith Barish, was pounding the drums for his film, proclaiming to an interviewer, ''This movie is like nothing anyone's seen on-screen in thirty years. It's got humor, drama, pathos.'' He was pushing it when he said the movie had ''humor,'' but he was right on target with ''drama'' and ''pathos.''

When *Ironweed* opened, *New York Times* film critic Janet Maslin wondered ''why audiences in the market for a big-budget Christmas film should be drawn to anything as downbeat and actionless as this one.'' Audiences weren't—at least not in large enough numbers to matter—

and the movie lost a bundle. On the other hand, it was a critical success, particularly for Nicholson and Streep. For instance, film critic Leonard Maltin, who found the movie "unremittingly bleak," also said, "The salvation is Nicholson and Streep, whose rich performances are a privilege to watch." The two stars of the film were honored with Oscar nominations (it was Nicholson's ninth!), but neither of them won.

Finally, in James L. Brooks's *Broadcast News*, which starred William Hurt, Holly Hunter, and Albert Brooks, the role of the network anchorman was played by Nicholson. You won't find his name in the credits; he offered to appear in several scenes at no charge in deference to the director who had helped him win his Oscar for *Terms of Endearment*. Brooks was equally appreciative, giving Nicholson some very choice, funny material.

Looking back on that extraordinary year, the New York Film Critics surprised no one when, citing all of his 1987 work, they named Nicholson Best Actor, giving him an unprecedented sixth acting award from that illustrious group.

By this point, Nicholson had been a movie actor for nearly thirty years, and had been involved in the production of forty-five films, as either a performer, writer, producer, and/or director. It seemed as if he had finally reached the very peak of his career. But there was another higher peak just ahead, waiting for him in Gotham City.

CHAPTER 20

"A One-Man Theater of Evil"

BATMAN OPENED IN movie theaters on the fiftieth anniversary of the caped crusader's first appearance in print in *Detective Comics No. 27.* Created by the then eighteen-year-old cartoonist Bob Kane, the character has become a part of our popular culture. And more so now than ever, thanks to the prodigious popularity of the 1989 *Batman* movie and its synergistic licensing success. At this writing, the film has already earned more than $250 million at the box office alone.

What a strange movie to have captured the public's fancy. It doesn't have the soul or warmth of *E.T. The Extra-Terrestrial,* the good-natured, action-a-minute swashbuckling of the *Indiana Jones* films, or the childlike energy and uplift of the *Star Wars* trilogy. No, this is a decidedly dark and moody movie, filled with violence, ugliness, and a lunatic sense of humor. But it works. And it works on two levels, as an action film and as a black comedy. The action falls to Batman (Michael Keaton), while the inspired psychotic comedy belongs strictly to the Joker (Nicholson). The action provides the plot and pacing of the movie. The humor pumps its black heart, giving it life.

It took ten years to bring *Batman* to the screen. There were countless obstacles, yet it was nearly made in the early 1980s with a $20 million budget. When it was ultimately produced, the movie cost more than $40 million, the largest percentage of which went to pay for the monumental set designed by Anton Furst. In fact, the set—five city blocks long—is the largest ever built since the 1963 budget colossus *Cleopatra*.

The look of the film was established even before the actors were cast. Nevertheless, producers Jon Peters and Peter Guber were well aware that the choices made for the leading roles would make or break their film.

The original thought was to hire an unknown to play Batman, in the fashion of Christopher Reeve, who played Superman. Later, some of the famous actors considered for Batman were Mel Gibson, Charlie Sheen, Pierce Brosnan, and Bill Murray. Though the producers claim otherwise, the presence of Bill Murray in that list suggests that at one point, at least, the tone of the film would have been much lighter—more like the original camp TV series of the 1960s starring Adam West.

And as for Adam West, the ex-Batman was miffed that he wasn't offered some sort of cameo role in the movie, perhaps playing Batman's father, or Commissioner Gordon. His inclusion in the cast might have been a sentimental choice, but the producers would not have any part of it. Their worst fear was that the production would be considered a retread of the old TV series, damning the film's hopes of pleasing the hard-core *Batman* comics fans who hated the TV series and who represented the audience the filmmakers most wanted to please.

At the same time they were trying to cast their Batman, the filmmakers were also hoping to land their arch villain, the Joker. So who did director Tim Burton and original screenwriter Sam Hamm consider for the pivotal role? "We thought," said Hamm, " 'Well, Willem Dafoe looks just like the Joker. David Bowie would be kind of neat because he's very funny when he does sinister roles. James Woods would be good and wouldn't need any makeup, which would save a couple of hours work every morning.' " But they kept coming back to the idea of Jack Nicholson.

Jon Peters had produced *The Witches of Eastwick*,

therefore the lines of communication were open to Jack. Nonetheless, when Nicholson was approached for the role, he was wary. No doubt he didn't want to get trapped in a mindless summer popcorn movie that would diminish his image as a serious actor. After all, playing Lex Luthor in *Superman* (1978) and *Superman II* (1980) tended to trivialize Gene Hackman in the eyes of many. It just so happened, though, that *Batman* had been one of Jackie Nicholson's favorite comic books when he was growing up in Neptune City, New Jersey. Like many kids, he preferred the caped crusader because, as he put it, Batman's power "was based on extended human skills rather than on superhuman skills or supernatural powers." The little boy was still very much alive in the adult Jack Nicholson. His interest was piqued.

Besides, Nicholson is intensely competitive. His old friend Warren Beatty had his own film based on a comic strip character (Dick Tracy) in the works for a very long time. This was a chance to beat him to the punch. But that would only be true, of course, if *Batman* was a hit.

There was clearly a lot to consider when Nicholson finally agreed to go to England to meet Tim Burton and talk about the film. After the meeting and a tour of the set, Nicholson kept his own counsel; he didn't say yes and he didn't say no. He'd think about it . . .

At the same time, the search for Batman intensified until one day Jon Peters suggested that Michael Keaton might be an inspired choice for the role. Having directed Keaton in *Beetlejuice* (1988), director Burton immediately saw the possibilities in such casting. The hard-core *Batman* fans back in the States, however, couldn't see it, imagine it, or stomach it. When the deal was announced, the comic book fans were horrified. They thought Keaton was a staggering error in judgment; to them, he was a lightweight comic actor of such films as *Mr. Mom*, not the semipsychotic dark knight of the contemporary Batman fable. Burton's answer was: "Comedy really does come from anger. Michael has this explosive side. All you have to do is look in his eyes and you know he's nuts.''

Protests mounted. Fifty thousand letters were written to denounce the casting of Keaton as Batman. The producers were frantic to stop the bad publicity. In addition to hiring Batman creator Bob Kane as a consultant, the producers did two things to try and stem the bad press. They released the now famous trailer for the film several months ahead of time, wowing the *Batman* crowd and assuaging some of their fears. And they went after Jack Nicholson with renewed fervor, knowing that they needed not only his talent, but his stature as an artist, to prove that their *Batman* was going to be a serious, top-drawer entertainment.

Nicholson reportedly was pleased with the hiring of Keaton to play Batman. To him, the gutsy move meant that the producers were going after something different, unique, special. But even as he was being wooed to play the Joker, one wonders if Nicholson was also thinking—in a very positive way—about the makeup he would have to wear for the role. Consider how he has so often chosen parts in his later years that have hidden his real face and frame. In both *Terms of Endearment* and *Prizzi's Honor* he was deliberately overweight. In *Ironweed* he played a derelict. What if he tried to look good and couldn't manage it? He has admitted to having difficulty keeping off the extra pounds, saying at one point that the only thing in his life that he's nostalgic for is his former weight. Could he be consciously (or unconsciously) avoiding that moment when the critics and the paying customers suddenly say, ''Jack Nicholson once played the devil, but now he looks like hell''? Or is he becoming, in the full flowering of his talent, more like the late Lord Laurence Olivier, an actor who took great delight in hiding behind false noses and such in order to lose himself entirely in his characters?

Whatever his reasons, Nicholson agreed to come on board—but at a very steep price. He was guaranteed top billing in the opening credits, paid $6 million up-front, and given a significant percentage of the revenue earned by the film *and* the licensing income! Most estimates put his probable take at $20 million, but some have suggested that he might actually clear as much as *$60 million* before every lunch box, T-shirt, videocassette, and poster has been sold.

Was Nicholson truly ideal for the role of the Joker? Media author Stephen Rebello writes, ''In 1980, Batman creator Bob Kane had sent a Warner Bros. executive, Roger Birnbaum, a doctored photo of Nicholson in Stanley Kubrick's film of Stephen King's *The Shining,* replete with green hair and whiteface.'' Kane never changed his mind; as far as he was concerned, Nicholson was always the Joker.

In Sam Hamm's original script, the Joker was the same age as Batman, thirty-two. Hamm was happy to rewrite. ''Nicholson can pull off basically anything, and he's going to give you shit you're not going to get if you cast somebody closer in age. If you get a star like Nicholson both for commercial and artistic reasons, it makes more sense to change the character.''

Once Nicholson was cast, there were other important decisions to be made. For instance, who would play Carl Grissom, Jack Napier's (the Joker's) criminal leader? Tim Burton said, ''Because Jack Nicholson is such a strong, cinematic figure, there aren't many you can imagine as his boss, but Jack Palance fills out the role perfectly, and is, in fact, able to make Nicholson look like a kid at times.''

The love interest, Vicki Vale, was another important role. Kim Basinger was the producers' first choice, but she had been unavailable. Sean Young was hired in her stead, but two weeks before filming started, Young broke her ankle in a riding mishap. Because filming had been moved back to accommodate Nicholson's schedule, Basinger was suddenly available again and immediately joined the cast. She was both an obvious and a dangerous choice. Long touted as the most desirable of all the female sex symbols in Hollywood, she had starred in an alarmingly endless string of box-office losers, from the steamy dud

9½ Weeks (1986) to the timid *My Stepmother Is an Alien* (1988). She had yet to fully click as a genuine star. *Batman* put her over the top. Some suggest that it may have also sent her over the edge (more on that later in the chapter).

Once filming began, Nicholson had to spend two hours per day having his Joker makeup applied. Wisely, though, they left Nicholson's incredibly expressive eyebrows untouched. And his killer smile was never put to more deadly use.

During the course of the grueling four-month shooting schedule, rumors of every description—most of them untrue—leaked out of the closed set. One of the reasons *Batman* was shot in London's Pinewood Studio was to avoid the intense scrutiny that might have attended the making of the film had it been shot in Hollywood. What the filmmakers didn't count on was the showing of the old *Batman* TV series on English television. Holy ratings, Batman, the show was a huge hit all over again, and Bat fever ran higher than ever right there in London. The Fleet Street tabloids knew a hot story when they saw one, they just had to find a way to get it. One paper, the *Daily Mail*, took shots of the secret set from a helicopter. Another paper, the *Sun*, was still more inventive, managing to slip a photographer onto the set for an exclusive, unauthorized photo essay.

There was the feeling of an armed camp about the *Batman* cast and crew. The paranoia surrounding the filmmakers was contagious. This was, after all, a very risky project. The film was intended to be Warner Bros.' big-budget blockbuster of the year; a lot of reputations would be tarnished if it failed. There were secrets to protect, and therefore, no one was supposed to talk to the press unless duly authorized, and there was no authorization given until the movie was nearly finished. In the meantime, though, the producers had given their okay to a small film team to make a documentary called *The Making of Batman*. Everyone cooperated with them—except Nicholson. He had agreed to be in *Batman*, nothing else. Besides, where was this little documentary going to be shown? In movie theaters? Not likely. Nicholson knew exactly where the film would end up: on television.

Jack Nicholson still doesn't do television!

Holding the line against the media was one thing, but rumors of a falling out between the director and Nicholson were something altogether different. When word of their feud hit the grapevine, the rumbles reached all the way to Hollywood. When asked about it, Burton said, "[Jack would] always question how much he should laugh as the Joker and, at one point, asked me if he could go really nuts in a scene. But that comes only when both have a clear idea of the proper approach to take. He wouldn't have asked that if he didn't feel we were in tune with each other." Later, Nicholson would say, "Every actor always worries if he's going over the top, but you couldn't do it in that part. There was no top."

In any event, Nicholson and Burton seemed well enough in tune for the actor to strut his way through some of the most memorable scenes of the 1980s, such as his animated discussion with a charred corpse and his wonderfully childish pique over the stealing of his poison gas balloons by Batman. As a means of bringing those and other scenes in the film to life, Nicholson used a "shorthand name" to get a fix on his character. He called the Joker "Velvet Death." He also played his character "short-wired. I'd do anything that came into my mind," he said.

While Nicholson was a brilliant choice to play the Joker, Michael Keaton made an ironic point. "You know," he said, "Jack's role of the Joker is much more similar to what I did in *Beetlejuice*. That role was so over the top that I just whaled on it." Though he didn't say so, the clear implication was that he could just as easily have played the Joker as Nicholson. And if he had, he could have avoided all the scorn and abuse heaped upon him from the diehard Batman fans before the movie finally opened and proved him up to the challenge of playing the film's dark hero.

* * *

In the months preceding the movie's opening, bat signals began springing up everywhere. By the time of the film's summer release, one could hardly avoid the ubiquitous gold and black images on billboards, T-shirts, hats, and so forth. Even if the film flopped, the marketing had already been firing on all cylinders. Though some believed that the movie had been overhyped and would suffer a backlash, it received generally glowing reviews and massive audience support.

When the reviews came in, Nicholson received just as much, if not more, attention than the film's title character, played by Keaton. *People* magazine said, "Jack Nicholson inhabited The Joker's role with such fevered invention that he stole the film." *Newsweek*'s Jack Kroll wrote, "Nicholson is a one-man theater of evil—he sings, he dances, he cracks wise, he kills and he enjoys every knife-ripping, bullet-riddling, acid-scarring minute of it."

Despite playing the villain, he was so colorful (beyond the green hair and purple zoot suit) and entertaining that Joker memorabilia sells in numbers nearly equaling those of Batman. In fact, Nicholson himself reportedly wears Joker T-shirts underneath his regular dress shirts, saying, "That nice green hair showing from under something else . . . that's a real fine fashion item." In keeping with his zany image, Jack spent some fifty thousand dollars on twenty-five shirts, six suits, six coats, and twelve hats in lurid shades of orange, turquoise, and purple that he wore in the movie.

Everyone loved Nicholson's performance. Everyone, that is, except the Academy of Motion Picture Arts and Sciences. To the surprise of many, his awe-inspiring performance in *Batman* did not receive an Oscar nomination. Adding insult to injury, the film received only one rather obvious nomination for Best Art Direction (by Anton Furst) but was ignored in every other category, including

Best Director, Best Costume Design, Best Special Effects, and Best Makeup, to name just a few that seemed like naturals.

There is one school of thought that says his fellow actors may have split their votes on Nicholson, some giving him the nod in the Best Supporting Actor category and others believing he deserved the Best Actor nomination. There is another school of thought that says that even if Nicholson's category were clear to the voters, he still wouldn't have been nominated because the film was too successful, and he personally made too much money. We're talking envy here. Either way you look at it, the Joker was robbed.

As soon as it was clear that *Batman* was a hit, talk immediately heated up about Hollywood's favorite kind of film: the sequel. (Note that the *Batman* sets were never torn down.)

In addition, speculation has run rampant as to who will replace Nicholson as the new villain. Some say Robin Williams will play the Riddler. Others say it will be Danny DeVito as the Penguin. Yet another camp says that you don't mess with a sure thing; bring back Jack Nicholson as the Joker. It doesn't seem to matter that he died rather convincingly at the end of the original film. Nevertheless, stranger things have happened. And just in case they do, Nicholson has reportedly announced that he'd reprise his role as the Joker for $24 million. It's clearly his way of saying, "I don't want to do this again, but if you pay me an exorbitant, ridiculous amount of money, hey, why not?"

Meanwhile, Nicholson has ascended to a new level of popularity that even he could never have imagined possible. In the past, he said that fan reaction was "pretty steady with me. If I go somewhere and I have to stand still, I collect your average celebrity crowd." He had long been a favorite of movie sophisticates, but he is no longer the youthful-looking heartthrob or hero who appeals to the teenage audience; yet he has nonetheless suddenly found himself an object of adulation by an army of young Joker fans. They seek him out and shout "Joker!" over and over again at the top of their lungs. They want autographs. They want to hear that maniacal laugh. They want Jack Nicholson to play the Joker forever. There are worse things to want.

Batman brought fame and fortune to a great many people connected to the hit film. The movie also spawned a curse upon its three major stars—one might call it the "*Batman* Scandal Curse"—that has seen Nicholson, Keaton, and Basinger become the objects of titillating sexual scandals that have landed all three of them in tabloid hell.

The *Batman* curse hit Nicholson first. His long relationship with Anjelica Huston was spoken of reverently by those who marveled at their warm, respectful, and loving seventeen-year union. This is not to say that Jack didn't have lovers on the side during those seventeen years, but he had been discreet, circumspect, and exceedingly low-key.

The *Batman* Scandal Curse ended that.

Not long after the movie struck gold at the box office, beautiful English sexpot and actress Karen Mayo-Chandler told *Playboy* magazine—in lurid detail—about her year-long affair with Nicholson, complete with handcuffs, whips, spankings, and Polaroid pictures. "All the things I like," said Karen, who met him on the Aspen ski slopes. To her, it was love—"He made me feel like a princess"—but to Jack, it was merely a wild sexual escapade. It only served to embarrass Anjelica and put a strain on their relationship.

What shocked Anjelica most was that Karen claimed to have spent the night with Nicholson on the eve of her father's funeral. "It is the last indignity I will suffer," she told a friend, yet somehow Nicholson managed to soothe Anjelica's feelings.

But not for long. The *Batman* Scandal Curse had barely begun to run its course.

On the heels of the *Playboy* story that described Nicholson's sexual predilections, another shocking news item hit the airwaves. Nicholson had gotten a twenty-six-year-old actress by the name of Rebecca Broussard pregnant, and she was going to have his baby. To make matters worse, Nicholson was said to have installed her in a $3 million home in Beverly Hills. He began taking her everywhere and spoke lovingly of the baby. Though marriage-shy for nearly twenty-five years, he even made noises about tying the knot with Rebecca after the baby was born.

Anjelica had had enough. She reportedly confronted him and hit him in the face. "Jack just went silent," said an observer. "He was destroyed. Anjelica had forgiven him time and time again for his affairs with young women. But when she learned he was about to become a father, it was the last straw."

Meanwhile, the curse struck Batman himself, Michael Keaton, when it was discovered that the married star had been carrying on an affair for two years with a striking blond beauty, Serina Robinson, whom he later learned was actually a porno star. Robinson made movies such as *Deep Obsession* and *Magic Sex Clinic* while working under assumed names. The result of the curse? The actor lost Robinson, whom he dropped like a hot coal, lost his wife, Caroline, who filed for divorce, and stands to lose more than $10 million when his divorce suit is finally settled.

The *Batman* curse works in mysterious ways. Consider Kim Basinger. Her scandal was, in some ways, the strangest of all. She fell madly in love with rock star and *Batman* composer Prince. Nothing wrong with that. Except Prince reportedly turned Basinger, Hollywood's hottest female sex symbol, into a veritable personal slave. "Kim is a very strong-willed person, but Prince's slightest wish is her command," said a friend. According to one report, she even clipped his toenails for him.

Prince's name had been linked with a string of talented

beauties, including singer Sheena Easton, and an insider warns: "When someone new catches his eye, away he goes. When it's over, it's over." And apparently that end has already come for Basinger.

CHAPTER 21

The Two Jakes

NICHOLSON COULDN'T let it go. What was it about *The Two Jakes* that consumed him so? The film was supposed to open for the 1989 Christmas season, qualifying it for Academy Award consideration. When Nicholson told Paramount that the film wouldn't be edited by then, the company rescheduled the premier for the Easter season of 1990. Nicholson told them in February that there was no way the movie would open in the spring. So Paramount bit the bullet again, finally releasing *The Two Jakes* on August 10, 1990, during the summer blockbuster season.

The movie was anything but a blockbuster. The long-awaited *Chinatown* sequel met a barrage of bad reviews and shockingly little interest at the box office. Kathleen Carroll of the *New York Daily News* spoke for many critics when she described the film as a "tedious experience." *The Two Jakes*, however, was not without its defenders. Reviewers Gene Siskel and Roger Ebert both gave it a thumbs-up, and *USA Today* raved, giving the movie three and a half stars. In the end, however, the film will probably be remembered as an ambitious failure.

Even before *Chinatown* was released to critical and commercial success back in 1974, Nicholson and the movie's screenwriter, Robert Towne, knew that they had something special. They decided then and there that *Chinatown* would be the first film in a trilogy that would use the character of detective Jake Gittes in an exploration of the dark side of modern Southern California history.

Chinatown was set in 1937. The second film in the trilogy, *The Two Jakes,* was intended to parallel real time; that is, it was to be set eleven years later (in 1948) and made in 1985, exactly eleven years after *Chinatown* was released. Obviously, the plan did not work out exactly as conceived. And therein lies a tale that is far more compelling than the movie itself.

In the mid 1980s, Nicholson, Towne, and *Chinatown* producer Robert Evans—all close friends—agreed to become equal partners, banking on their collective talents to turn *The Two Jakes* into as big a hit as *Chinatown* had been. Towne would write and direct the film, Nicholson would reprise his role of Jake Gittes, and Evans would produce, as well as play the second Jake (Jake Berman, the villain). The partners cut a deal with Paramount Pictures that called for no salaries up-front but a major slice of the box-office receipts. Next, they established a company called T.E.N. Productions, the initials standing for Towne, Evans, and Nicholson, and then spun off a subsidiary called Two Jakes Productions. They obviously had big plans beyond this one movie.

Evans, who had begun his Hollywood career as an actor in the 1950s before becoming the head of production at Paramount (and producing such hits as *The Godfather*) had decided to resurrect his acting career with *The Two Jakes* after a twenty-five-year hiatus from the big screen. It was his participation as an actor in the film that set the wheels of destruction in motion.

The movie was supposed to begin shooting in early 1985. Towne, as the writer/director, was liable to Paramount for cost overruns. During the preproduction process he became convinced that Evans was incapable of playing the part of the second Jake and wanted to fire him. It was a sticky situation. How does a director fire his producer? Especially when they're partners and best friends. Nicholson was caught in the middle of the turmoil; friendship and loyalty are *el primo* with him, and he suddenly found himself in the uncomfortable position of having to be loyal to either one or the other. There was no middle ground. As reported by Ivor Davis in *Los Angeles* magazine, in the end, Nicholson opted to side with Evans, figuring that it was only a movie, and in the acting arena, perhaps he could coach Evans or use some tricks to make him look good. He appealed to Towne, saying, ''Bob used to run Paramount . . . You can't treat him like a piece of shit. You have to show respect.''

Nicholson was no Goody Two-Shoes. He knew how the game was played. He didn't rise up out of the B-movie wasteland and become a star by letting things happen *to* him. He made things happen to *other* people. In this case, he wanted Towne to start shooting the film. It was his idea to get a couple of weeks of footage in the can, committing Paramount financially to the movie, so that it would really cost them a bundle to bail out. He explained to Towne that Robert Evans's scenes didn't have to be shot right away. When that point came, said Nicholson, they'd give Evans a few days to show what he could do. If he stunk up the picture, *then,* said Nicholson, he'd back Towne up and suggest that Evans drop out of the movie. And seeing that he was bad, perhaps Evans would not even put up a fight, suggested Nicholson. Okay, he conceded, so they'd have to throw out a few days worth of film—but it was better than not getting the movie made at all, because that's what would happen, predicted Nicholson, if Towne tried to fire Evans before the movie began filming.

Towne refused to go along with Nicholson's plan. He wanted Evans out of the film then and there. Evans, outraged, refused to quit.

The Two Jakes production ground to a halt. Lawyers were called in by Paramount to devise a new agreement that called upon all three partners to be equally liable for any cost overruns. Towne and Evans agreed and signed the document. Nicholson felt he was being set up. Towne didn't have the kind of money Nicholson had, and Evans had lost a fortune on *The Cotton Club* (1984) and had been implicated (though not indicted) in a murder case stemming from that film. He didn't have deep pockets, either. In other words, Nicholson was the one who would have to pay if anything went wrong with the film. He was taking all the risk for only one-third of the potential gain.

The actor put his foot down and refused to sign the new agreement. Though he had been the one trying to save the movie, his action was the one that actually killed *The Two Jakes*. Paramount flushed it.

A great deal of money—more than one million dollars—had already been spent on sets, antique automobiles, costumes, and so forth, and somebody had to pay for it all. Nicholson was soon elected the mayor of lawsuit city.

In the aftershock of the debacle, he took the high road, saying, "These were two of my oldest friends, and we had some problems among ourselves. Hey, we had some words, but these are guys who have words anyway. The sad thing is, it's our own goddamn fault. We blew higher than a kite over some pretty minor issues, and we got ourselves too close to a deadline, and we can't be mad at Paramount for that."

It was certainly obvious that Nicholson wasn't mad at Paramount. As soon as *The Two Jakes* bit the dust, he did the studio a huge favor by stepping into the Mike Nichols project *Heartburn* when the film was already two weeks into production.

Several years passed, and Nicholson's clout in the industry continued to grow. He had two more Oscar nominations, plus a major hit with *The Witches of Eastwick*, and an anticipated blockbuster with *Batman*. Throughout those years, Nicholson refused to abandon *The Two Jakes*. The script was too good, his role was too rich, and the potential too great to pass up the opportunity of getting the movie made. He tried everything, including asking his old pal Warren Beatty to produce as well as costar as the second Jake. He went to Roman Polanski, the original director of *Chinatown*. He had acted in three Mike Nichols films, the last one, *Heartburn*, as a favor. He asked for the favor in return: Would Nichols direct *The Two*

Jakes? Nope. He tried Bernardo Bertolucci, with whom he had hoped to make *Red Harvest* in the early 1980s. That didn't work out. He even turned to his father figure, John Huston, but the great director, who had acted so wonderfully in *Chinatown,* didn't want to take on the troubled project.

Nicholson was like a dog chewing on a bone; he wouldn't give it up.

Finally, after Paramount settled all the outstanding lawsuits, compromises were worked out that suddenly breathed new life into the moribund project. Both Towne and Evans needed this movie made. Besides the original fiasco in 1985, Towne had failed twice as a director, with *Personal Best* and *Tequila Sunrise.* Evans was still enmeshed in the ''Cotton Club murder case'' and had to salvage his producing career. All agreed that Nicholson was the key player. Without him, there was no movie. So both Towne and Evans gave ground, each giving up what they wanted most. Towne gave up directing the film, and Evans agreed not to act in it.

The Two Jakes was back on track, getting the extra (much-needed) positive publicity of having Nicholson work as the film's director as well as its star. He was taking a big risk. This jinxed film's success or failure now rested squarely on his shoulders; he was putting his prestige and status directly on the line.

That's what got the movie shot, but that might also have been why the movie was so long in the editing process. New scenes were being shot as late as July for the August release. Another problem was the strain on the relationship between Nicholson and Towne. After six months of rewrites, the screenwriter took a long vacation on Bora Bora and then became involved in writing the script for *Days of Thunder,* starring Tom Cruise. Towne was unavailable to Nicholson during a crucial time, and the actor/director ultimately rewrote part of the script himself, most notably adding the narration that many believe to be the best part of the film.

* * *

Nicholson replaced Bob Evans as Jake Berman with Harvey Keitel. And sharing producing duties with Evans was Nicholson's trusted friend Harold Schneider, who produced *Goin' South.* He also put his daughter, Jennifer, on the payroll as an assistant production designer. She even pulled duty as an extra.

While *Chinatown* dealt with the issue of water rights, *The Two Jakes* took on the corruption of the California oil patch. But much changed in the eleven years since Gittes failed to stop the evil he saw in Chinatown. He fought in World War II. In the new film, he's mellower, easier on himself after all he's seen and done. The man has even joined a country club. When we see Jake Gittes, we see the changes in his face and his body. We also see the old scars, particularly the one on the left side of his nose where a punk cut open his nostril back in '37. Gittes, however, tries not to look back. It's the postwar boom years, and Southern California is growing. Money is being made. But when somebody wants more than their share—and kills for it—Gittes is back in action.

Robert Towne created Jake Gittes in Jack Nicholson's image. Perhaps that accounts for why the actor has been so intense about making *The Two Jakes.* The Joker and Darryl Van Horne were fun. Charley Partanna was a change of pace. But Gittes is very close to him; they have much in common, both on the surface and deep within their psyches. For instance, both Jake (in the postwar film) and Jack are passionate about clothes. The strong sense of personal power, bordering on arrogance, that Nicholson possesses is also part of Gittes's character. And even Nicholson's sly, low-key, manipulative style of using jokes to cajole for what he wants, coupled with his sometimes explosive temper, is also there in the character of Gittes.

All these elements may be part and parcel of both Gittes and Nicholson, but directing himself has had its drawbacks. "I'm flat about twenty-five percent more of the time than I would be if I had another director looking after me," he confided. "But you don't get flat in a great scene. And I don't think I'm a dead man because the dailies are bad. I can always dub a line later. The great advantage is, I don't have to ask the director, 'Do you mind if I drop down here and block that actor's face?'"

Comparisons to *Chinatown* were inevitable. For his part, Nicholson admitted, "I'm not Roman Polanski. But," he quickly added, "I'd be doing the same thing as an actor if he were directing, and I think he'd be doing the same things as a director."

After he failed to win critical and public acceptance for *Drive, He Said* and *Goin' South,* this third stab at directing was crucial to Nicholson's future filmmaking hopes. His critical and commercial failure may finally close the door to future directorial efforts. That would be a cruel fate, because Nicholson has a great deal of respect for the industry's better directors, and nothing would please him more than to be considered one of their kind. He may, instead, have to be satisfied with being known as the greatest Hollywood actor of his time.

CHAPTER 22

The One Jack

JACK NICHOLSON'S professional life has never been richer or more rewarding than during the last several years. But during this same period, his personal life, without Anjelica, has taken a decided turn for the worse. Unlike many past assignations, his affairs with Karen Mayo-Chandler and Rebecca Broussard have made worldwide headlines. Those affairs also shattered the fragile stability of his world outside the movie business.

It's ironic that Jack and Anjelica had never seemed closer and more comfortable with each other than during the aftermath of her success in *Prizzi's Honor*. His relationship with her and her father had reached a satisfying creative fruition, and her subsequent Best Supporting Actress Oscar was a source of great pride to Nicholson. Their relationship apparently began to change not long afterward. Anjelica spent less and less time with Nicholson as she became more active as an actress, with leading roles in such prestigious productions as her father's *The Dead* (1987), the TV miniseries *Lonesome Dove* (1988), Woody Allen's *Crimes and Misdemeanors* (1989), and Paul Mazursky's *Enemies, A Love Story* (1989), the last of which brought her another Oscar nomination for Best Supporting Actress.

According to Karen Mayo-Chandler, it was during Anjelica's ascendancy as an actress that the British bombshell spent close to twelve months in a hot and heavy sexual relationship with Nicholson. The actor, famous for both giving and receiving nicknames, had yet another one tagged on him by Karen: "Spanking Jack."

There is more than a touch of irony in Nicholson's relationship with Mayo-Chandler. She, like Mimi Machu and Anjelica, had been a model—and a rather successful one, at that, having graced the covers of more than one hundred fashion magazines. Most interesting of all, however, is her connection to Nicholson's own past. She has been working steadily in B movies, acting, in one instance, alongside old Nicholson heartthrob actress Karen Black, and she has even signed for a five-picture deal with Nicholson's mentor, Roger Corman.

Mayo-Chandler's kiss-and-tell rendition of life in the sack with Nicholson was, in its way, rather complimentary to the star. She was quite explicit about his sexual prowess, suggesting that he write a book called *How to Make Love To a Woman*.

The British starlet acknowledged she knew that Nicholson has had a long-term relationship with Anjelica Huston. She was under the distinct impression, though, that "their relationship had become a friendship thing by that time." Nonetheless, she noted that the actor kept a picture of Anjelica in, of all places, the bathroom.

The kiss-and-tell actress insisted that she told Jack of her plan to go public with their affair. The London tabloids, she claimed, had begun painting her as "Jack's little British bimbo." She no doubt reasoned that if the story was already breaking in the press, why not tell it from her own point of view? But would she be breaking a confidence with Nicholson if she did so? In her rendition of their talk, after she told Jack that she was going to tell all, he said he didn't mind, that the publicity would be good for both of them. One wonders, though, if he knew she was going to say, "Jack's a very noisy love-maker when he gets going, a real grunter, and he likes a lot of verbal encouragement, too."

Nicholson is on public record as saying, "By nature, I am not monogamous . . . I say monogamy doesn't make any difference; women suspect you whether it's true or not.'' In any event, it is generally understood that Anjelica knew about and tolerated Jack's infidelities. After all, they hadn't lived together since the early 1980s. Still, there was a strong bond between them that meant more than a shared roof or a wedding ring. They had talked about having children together. Nicholson has been quoted time and time again about his desire to have kids. He hadn't been involved in the raising of his daughter, Jennifer, because she grew up in Hawaii; he felt he had missed out on something very important. Anjelica seemed to be warming to the concept of motherhood when she told an interviewer, ''Thirty-six always occurred to me as the year I would have a child.'' She didn't.

In a seemingly lighthearted vein, Nicholson once said, ''I'm always going around trying to have babies.'' Well, he finally succeeded. Actress Rebecca Broussard, who plays Nicholson's secretary in *The Two Jakes,* gave him a little girl, Lorraine, who was born in April 1990.

Nicholson met the twenty-six-year-old actress when she was working as a waitress at a popular Los Angeles restaurant. Their relationship began in June 1988, fast upon his return from England, where he had made *Batman.* Soon thereafter he was involved with both *The Two Jakes* and Rebecca. About fifteen months later, she announced that she was pregnant and that she wanted to keep the child.

Outspokenly antiabortion, Nicholson was apparently delighted to become a parent, but flat out said he would not marry Rebecca, although at one point he seemed to toy with the idea. In any event, he reportedly has promised to support both the mother and the child. And it is fair to say that he will likely take an active role in the baby's life.

But what of the real love of his life? Though bitterly hurt by recent events, Anjelica Huston has kept her dignity. Though women like Mayo-Chandler have come and gone in Nicholson's life and have been, at worst, a relatively minor threat to Anjelica's relationship with Jack, Broussard is different. By virtue of having Nicholson's baby, both she and the child will be a part of Jack's life forever.

"I don't want to hurt anybody," Nicholson said plaintively. "Why can't we all be friends? I want to be good to everyone, but the situation is driving me nuts." According to one source, Nicholson is "absolutely lost without Anjelica. He's devastated that she refused to take him back." He has reportedly been sending her a slew of expensive presents, but she returns them all, unopened.

After the failure of *The Two Jakes* and the apparent end of his relationship with Anjelica, Nicholson has come to a major crossroads. That he will give great screen performances in the years ahead is a foregone conclusion. Whether he will be happy in his personal life is another question altogether.

But then, Nicholson once said, "I live my life on a simple kind of code. Anything I do is in the open. In that way, I'm not ashamed to admit anything I've done at any time or in any place." To a remarkable degree, Nicholson has lived by that code. He might be an eccentric, womanizing rebel, but he's never been a hypocrite. While he may have made any number of mistakes that he deeply regrets, his honesty, in both his on-screen performances and in his personal relationships, has been his hallmark.

If honesty is his hallmark, then loyalty is his flag of honor. We have talked much about his loyalty to friends, but his greatest loyalty has been to his work. There hasn't been another movie star in the last twenty years who has so often and so consistently changed, grown, and risked failure (often dodging the bullet) in the search of creative excellence.

Nicholson was heralded in the early 1970s as the actor of the decade. He has been so much more. He has been the actor and the image of our times: alienated yet full of a mercurial energy that makes anything possible. He is both hero and villain—and always the most mesmerizing presence in any movie in which he appears. Meryl Streep once called him ''the Mick Jagger of motion pictures.'' We'll let that stand.

APPENDIX A

Nicholson and Oscar

As of this writing, Nicholson has had nine Academy Award nominations, three for Best Supporting Actor, winning once, and six for Best Actor, taking Oscar home once in that illustrious category, as well.

1969
Best Supporting Actor Nominees

Rupert Crosse in *The Reivers*
Elliott Gould in *Bob & Carol & Ted & Alice*
JACK NICHOLSON in *Easy Rider*
Anthony Quayle in *Anne of the Thousand Days*
*Gig Young in *They Shoot Horses, Don't They?*

1970
Best Actor Nominees

Melvyn Douglas in *I Never Sang for My Father*
James Earl Jones in *The Great White Hope*
JACK NICHOLSON in *Five Easy Pieces*
Ryan O'Neal in *Love Story*
*George C. Scott in *Patton*

*Denotes winner

1973
Best Actor Nominees

Marlon Brando in *Last Tango in Paris*
*Jack Lemmon in *Save the Tiger*
JACK NICHOLSON in *The Last Detail*
Al Pacino in *Serpico*
Robert Redford in *The Sting*

1974
Best Actor Nominees

*Art Carney in *Harry and Tonto*
Albert Finney in *Murder on the Orient Express*
Dustin Hoffman in *Lenny*
JACK NICHOLSON in *Chinatown*
Al Pacino in *The Godfather, Part II*

1975
Best Actor Nominees

Walter Matthau in *The Sunshine Boys*
*JACK NICHOLSON in *One Flew Over the Cuckoo's Nest*
Al Pacino in *Dog Day Afternoon*
Maximilian Schell in *The Man in the Glass Booth*
James Whitmore in *Give 'em Hell, Harry!*

1981
Best Supporting Actor Nominees

James Coco in *Only When I Laugh*
*John Gielgud in *Arthur*
Ian Holm in *Chariots of Fire*
JACK NICHOLSON in *Reds*
Howard E. Rollins, Jr., in *Ragtime*

1983
Best Supporting Actor Nominees

Charles Durning in *To Be or Not to Be*
John Lithgow in *Terms of Endearment*
*JACK NICHOLSON in *Terms of Endearment*
Sam Shepard in *The Right Stuff*
Rip Torn in *Cross Creek*

1985
Best Actor Nominees

Harrison Ford in *Witness*
James Garner in *Murphy's Romance*
*William Hurt in *Kiss of the Spider Woman*
JACK NICHOLSON in *Prizzi's Honor*
Jon Voight in *Runaway Train*

1987
Best Actor Nominees

*Michael Douglas in *Wall Street*
William Hurt in *Broadcast News*
Marcello Mastroianni in *Dark Eyes*
JACK NICHOLSON in *Ironweed*
Robin Williams in *Good Morning, Vietnam*

APPENDIX B

Roles He Might Have Played

It's always fascinating to consider the choices an actor makes in his career. Had Rip Torn not quit the cast of *Easy Rider,* where would Jack Nicholson be today? Where would Rip Torn be? Below is a short list of some of the possibilities that confronted Jack Nicholson during the last two decades. When a reason for the choice is known, it's included. Often, busy stars turn down roles that they would love to play simply because production schedules don't mesh with previous commitments; that may be the case in a number of the examples below for which no reason is given.

The Godfather (1972), the Al Pacino role. Nicholson later joked that he thought he had to be Italian to play Michael Corleone.

The Sting (1973), the Robert Redford role. Nicholson said, "I like the period setting, the whole project, and I know it will be commercial. But I need to put my energies into a movie that really needs them. I need to take a risk." He chose, instead, *The Last Detail.*

The Great Gatsby (1974), the Robert Redford role. Nicholson reportedly asked for too much money and bid himself out of the running.

Coming Home (1978), the Jon Voight role. Reason for turning it down unknown.

Apocalypse Now (1979), the Martin Sheen role. Apparently, like so many others who refused the role, he didn't want to spend six months in the Philippine jungle. Besides, he had been to the Philippines to make his own movies in the 1960s.

China Syndrome (1979), the Oscar-nominated Jack Lemmon role. Reason for turning it down unknown.

Red Harvest (unproduced). Nicholson had agreed to star in director Bernardo Bertolucci's version of Dashiell Hammett's novel of the same name, but the deal fell apart in 1984.

The Untouchables (1987), the Kevin Costner role. Reason for turning it down unknown.

APPENDIX C

Jack Nicholson Filmography

1958
Cry Baby Killer

Starring:	Harry Lauter, JACK NICHOLSON, Carolyn Mitchell, Brett Halsey, Lynn Cartwright
Director:	Jus Addis
Producer:	Roger Corman
Screenplay:	Leo Gordon and Melvin Levy

1960
Little Shop of Horrors

Starring:	Jonathan Haze, Jackie Joseph, Mel Welles, Dick Miller, Myrtle Vail, Leola Wendorff, JACK NICHOLSON
Director:	Roger Corman
Producer:	Roger Corman
Screenplay:	Charles B. Griffith

1960
Too Soon to Love

Starring:	Jennifer West, Richard Evans, Warren Parker, Ralph Manza, JACK NICHOLSON
Director:	Richard Rush
Producer:	Mark Lipsky
Screenplay:	Lazlo Gorog and Richard Rush

1960
Studs Lonigan

Starring: Christopher Knight, Frank Gorshin,
               Venetia Stevenson, Carolyn Craig,
               JACK NICHOLSON, Robert Caspar, Dick
               Foran, Jay C. Flippen, Kathy Johnson
Director: Irving Lerner
Producer: Philip Yordan
Screenplay: Philip Yordan

1960
The Wild Ride

Starring: JACK NICHOLSON, Georgianna Carter,
               Robert Bean
Director: Harvey Berman
Producer: Harvey Berman
Screenplay: Ann Porter and Marion Rothman

1962
The Broken Land

Starring: Kent Taylor, Dianna Darrin,
               Jody McCrea, Robert Sampson,
               JACK NICHOLSON, Gary Snead
Director: John Bushelman
Producer: Leonard Schwartz
Screenplay: Edward Lakso

1963
The Raven

Starring: Vincent Price, Peter Lorre, Boris Karloff,
               Hazel Court, Olive Sturgess,
               JACK NICHOLSON, Connie Wallace,
               William Baskin, Aaron Saxon
Director: Roger Corman
Producer: Roger Corman
Screenplay: Richard Matheson

1963
The Terror

Starring:	Boris Karloff, JACK NICHOLSON, Sandra Knight, Richard Miller, Dorothy Neumann, Jonathan Haze
Director:	Roger Corman
Producer:	Roger Corman
Screenplay:	Leo Gordon and Jack Hill

1963
Thunder Island

Starring:	Gene Nelson, Fay Spain, Briany Kelly, Miriam Colon, Art Bedard, Antonio Torres Martino
Director:	Jack Leewood
Producer:	Jack Leewood
Screenplay:	JACK NICHOLSON and Don Devlin

1964
Ensign Pulver

Starring:	Robert Walker, Jr., Burl Ives, Walter Matthau, Millie Perkins, Tommy Sands, Kay Medford, Larry Hagman, Gerald O'Laughlin, Sal Papa, Al Freeman, Jr., James Farentino, James Coco, Diana Sands, JACK NICHOLSON
Director:	Joshua Logan
Producer:	Joshua Logan
Screenplay:	Joshua Logan and Thomas Heggen

1964
Back Door To Hell

Starring:	Jimmie Rodgers, JACK NICHOLSON, John Hackett, Annabelle Huggins
Director:	Monte Hellman
Producer:	Fred Roos
Screenplay:	Richard Guttman and John Hackett

1966
Flight To Fury

Starring:	Dewey Martin, Fay Spain, JACK NICHOLSON, Jacqueline Hellman, Vic Diaz, Joseph Estrada, John Hackett
Director:	Monte Hellman
Producer:	Fred Roos
Screenplay:	JACK NICHOLSON

1966
The Shooting

Starring:	Warren Oates, Will Hutchins, Millie Perkins, JACK NICHOLSON, B. J. Merholz
Director:	Monte Hellman
Producer:	Monte Hellman and JACK NICHOLSON
Screenplay:	Carol Eastman writing as Adrien Joyce

1966
Ride in the Whirlwind

Starring:	Cameron Mitchell, JACK NICHOLSON, Millie Perkins, Tom Fuler, Katherine Squire, George Mitchell, Brandon Caroll
Director:	Monte Hellman
Producer:	Monte Hellman and JACK NICHOLSON
Screenplay:	JACK NICHOLSON

1967
Hell's Angels on Wheels

Starring: JACK NICHOLSON, Adam Rourke,
Sabrina Scharf, Jana Taylor, John
Garwood, Richard Anders, I. J. Jefferson
Director: Richard Rush
Producer: Joe Solomon
Screenplay: R. Wright Campbell

1967
Rebel Rousers

Starring: Cameron Mitchell, JACK NICHOLSON,
Bruce Dern, Diane Ladd,
Harry Dean Stanton
Director: Martin B. Cohen
Producer: Martin B. Cohen
Screenplay: Abe Polsky, Michael Kars, and Martin B.
Cohen

1967
The St. Valentine's Day Massacre

Starring: Jason Robards, George Segal, Ralph
Meeker, Jean Hale, Clint Ritchie, Frank
Silvera, Joseph Campanella, Richard
Bakalyan, David Canary, Bruce Dern,
Harold J. Stone, John Agar,
JACK NICHOLSON
Director: Roger Corman
Producer: Roger Corman
Screenplay: Howard Browne

1967
The Trip

Starring:	Peter Fonda, Susan Strasberg, Bruce Dern, Dennis Hopper
Director:	Roger Corman
Producer:	Roger Corman
Screenplay:	JACK NICHOLSON

1968
Psych-Out

Starring:	Susan Strasberg, Dean Stockwell, JACK NICHOLSON, Bruce Dern, Adam Rourke, Max Julien, Henry Jaglom, I. J. Jefferson
Director:	Richard Rush
Producer:	Dick Clark
Screenplay:	E. Hunter Willett and Betty Ulius

1968
Head

Starring:	The Monkees, Victor Mature, Annette Funicello, and featuring Frank Zappa, Carol Doda, Sonny Liston, I. J. Jefferson
Director:	Bob Rafelson
Producer:	Bob Rafelson and JACK NICHOLSON
Screenplay:	Bob Rafelson and JACK NICHOLSON

1969
Easy Rider

Starring:	Peter Fonda, Dennis Hopper, JACK NICHOLSON
Director:	Dennis Hopper
Producer:	Peter Fonda
Screenplay:	Peter Fonda, Dennis Hopper, and Terry Southern

1970
On a Clear Day You Can See Forever

Starring: Barbra Streisand, Yves Montand,
               Bob Newhart, Larry Blyden,
               JACK NICHOLSON, Simon Oakland
Director: Vincente Minnelli
Producer: Howard Koch
Screenplay: Alan J. Lerner

1970
Five Easy Pieces

Starring: JACK NICHOLSON, Karen Black,
               Lois Smith, Susan Anspach
Director: Bob Rafelson
Producer: Bob Rafelson and Richard Weschler
Screenplay: Carol Eastman writing as Adrien Joyce

1970
Drive, He Said

Starring: William Tepper, Karen Black, Michael
               Margotta, Bruce Dern, Robert Towne,
               Henry Jaglom, June Fairchild
Director: JACK NICHOLSON
Producer: JACK NICHOLSON and Steve Blauner
Screenplay: JACK NICHOLSON and Jeremy Larner

1971
A Safe Place

Starring: Tuesday Weld, JACK NICHOLSON,
               Orson Welles, Philip Proctor,
               Gwen Welles
Director: Henry Jaglom
Producer: Bert Schneider
Screenplay: Henry Jaglom

1971
Carnal Knowledge

Starring: JACK NICHOLSON, Candice Bergen,
                Art Garfunkel, Ann-Margret, Rita
                Moreno, Cynthia O'Neal, Carol Kane
Director: Mike Nichols
Producer: Mike Nichols
Screenplay: Jules Feiffer

1972
The King of Marvin Gardens

Starring: JACK NICHOLSON, Bruce Dern,
                Ellen Burstyn, Julia Anne Robinson,
                Scatman Crothers
Director: Bob Rafelson
Producer: Bob Rafelson
Screenplay: Jacob Brackman

1973
The Last Detail

Starring: JACK NICHOLSON, Otis Young,
                Randy Quaid, Clifton James, Carol Kane,
                Michael Moriarty, Luana Anders
Director: Hal Ashby
Producer: Gerald Ayres
Screenplay: Robert Towne

1974
Chinatown

Starring: JACK NICHOLSON, Faye Dunaway,
                John Huston, Perry Lopez, Diane Ladd,
                Darrell Zwerling, John Hillerman,
                Roman Polanski
Director: Roman Polanski
Producer: Robert Evans
Screenplay: Robert Towne

1975
The Passenger

Starring:	JACK NICHOLSON, Maria Schneider
Director:	Michelangelo Antonioni
Producer:	Carlo Ponti
Screenplay:	Mark Peloe, Peter Wollen, and Michelangelo Antonioni

1975
Tommy

Starring:	Ann-Margret, Roger Daltry, Oliver Reed, Elton John, Keith Moon, JACK NICHOLSON, Eric Clapton, Robert Powell, The Who
Director:	Ken Russell
Producer:	Ken Russell and Robert Stigwood
Screenplay:	Ken Russell

1975
The Fortune

Starring:	JACK NICHOLSON, Warren Beatty, Stockard Channing
Director:	Mike Nichols
Producer:	Hank Moonjean
Screenplay:	Carol Eastman writing as Adrien Joyce

1975
One Flew Over the Cuckoo's Nest

Starring:	JACK NICHOLSON, Louise Fletcher, William Redfield, Will Sampson, Brad Dourif, Marya Small, Louisa Moritz, Sydney Lassick, Scatman Crothers, Danny DeVito, Dr. Dean Brooks
Director:	Milos Forman
Producer:	Saul Zaentz and Michael Douglas
Screenplay:	Lawrence Hauben and Bo Goldman

1976
The Missouri Breaks

Starring:	Marlon Brando, JACK NICHOLSON, Randy Quaid, Kathleen Lloyd, Frederic Forrest, Harry Dean Stanton, John McLiam
Director:	Arthur Penn
Producer:	Robert M. Sherman
Screenplay:	Thomas McGuane

1976
The Last Tycoon

Starring:	Robert DeNiro, Ingrid Boulting, Robert Mitchum, Jeanne Moreau, JACK NICHOLSON, Tony Curtis, Donald Pleasence, Ray Milland, Dana Andrews, Theresa Russell
Director:	Elia Kazan
Producer:	Sam Spiegel
Screenplay:	Harold Pinter

1979
Goin' South

Starring:	JACK NICHOLSON, Mary Steenburgen, Christopher Lloyd, John Belushi, Veronica Cartwright, Richard Bradford, Jeff Morris
Director:	JACK NICHOLSON
Producer:	Harry Gittes and Harold Schneider
Screenplay:	John Herman Shareer, Al Ramus, Charles Shyer, and Alan Mandel

1980
The Shining

Starring: JACK NICHOLSON, Shelley Duvall,
               Danny Lloyd, Scatman Crothers,
               Barry Nelson, Philip Stone, Joe Turkel
Director: Stanley Kubrick
Producer: Stanley Kubrick
Screenplay: Stanley Kubrick and Diane Johnson

1981
The Postman Always Rings Twice

Starring: JACK NICHOLSON, Jessica Lange,
               John Colicos, Michael Lerner, John Ryan,
               Anjelica Huston, Jon Van Ness
Director: Bob Rafelson
Producer: Bob Rafelson and Charles Mulvehill
Screenplay: David Mamet

1981
Reds

Starring: Warren Beatty, Diane Keaton,
               JACK NICHOLSON, Edward Herrmann,
               Jerzy Kosinski, Paul Sorvino, Maureen
               Stapleton, Nicolas Coster, Ian Wolfe,
               Bessie Love, Gene Hackman
Director: Warren Beatty
Producer: Warren Beatty
Screenplay: Warren Beatty and Trevor Griffiths

1981
The Border

Starring:	JACK NICHOLSON, Valerie Perrine, Harvey Keitel, Warren Oates, Elpidia Carillo, Shannon Wilcox
Director:	Tony Richardson
Producer:	Edgar Bronfman
Screenplay:	Deric Washburn, Walon Green, and David Freeman

1983
Terms of Endearment

Starring:	Shirley MacLaine, Debra Winger, JACK NICHOLSON, Jeff Daniels, Danny DeVito, John Lithgow, Kate Charleson, Lisa Hart Carroll
Director:	James L. Brooks
Producer:	James L. Brooks
Screenplay:	James L. Brooks

1985
Prizzi's Honor

Starring:	JACK NICHOLSON, Kathleen Turner, Anjelica Huston, William Hickey, John Randolph, Lee Richardson, Robert Loggia, Michael Lombard
Director:	John Huston
Producer:	John Foreman
Screenplay:	Richard Condon and Janet Roach

1986
Heartburn

Starring:	Meryl Streep, JACK NICHOLSON, Jeff Daniels, Maureen Stapleton, Stockard Channing, Richard Masur, Catherine O'Hara, Steven Hill, Milos Forman, Natalie Stern, Karen Akers
Director:	Mike Nichols
Producer:	Mike Nichols and Robert Greenhut
Screenplay:	Nora Ephron

1987
The Witches of Eastwick

Starring:	JACK NICHOLSON, Cher, Susan Sarandon, Michelle Pfeiffer, Veronica Cartwright, Richard Jenkins, Keith Jochim, Carel Struycken
Director:	George Miller
Producer:	Neil Canton, Peter Guber, Jon Peters
Screenplay:	Michael Cristofer

1987
Broadcast News

Starring:	William Hurt, Albert Brooks, Holly Hunter, Robert Prosky, Lois Chiles, Joan Cusack, Peter Hackes, JACK NICHOLSON
Director:	James L. Brooks
Producer:	James L. Brooks
Screenplay:	James L. Brooks

1987
Ironweed

Starring:	JACK NICHOLSON, Meryl Streep, Carroll Baker, Michael O'Keefe, Diane Venora, Fred Gwynne, Margaret Whitton, Tom Waits, Jake Dengel, Joe Grifasi
Director:	Hector Babenco
Producer:	Joseph H. Kanter, Denis Blouin, Rob Cohen
Screenplay:	William Kennedy

1989
Batman

Starring:	JACK NICHOLSON, Michael Keaton, Kim Basinger, Jack Palance, Robert Wuhl, Billy Dee Williams, Pat Hingle, Jerry Hall, Michael Gough, Lee Wallace, Tracey Walter
Director:	Tim Burton
Producer:	Jon Peters and Peter Guber
Screenplay:	Sam Hamm and Warren Skaaren

1990
The Two Jakes

Starring:	JACK NICHOLSON, Harvey Keitel, Meg Tilly, Madeleine Stowe, Eli Wallach, Frederic Forrest, Richard Farnsworth, Ruben Blades, David Keith
Director:	JACK NICHOLSON
Producer:	Robert Evans and Harold Schneider
Screenplay:	Robert Towne

REFERENCES

INTRODUCTION

"I've been at parties where Jack . . ." *Jack Nicholson: Face to Face,* Richard David Crane and Christopher Fryer, M. Evans and Co., Inc., 1975.

"I know that if I were in a trouble situation . . ." Paul Attanasio, *Washington Post,* June 14, 1985.

CHAPTER 1

"I never really had a relationship . . ." *Playboy,* 1972.

"because my environment . . ." *Screw,* 1972.

"We tried to talk about everything . . ." *Family Weekly,* January 7, 1973.

"Someone called me on the phone . . ." Nancy Collins, *Rolling Stone,* March 29, 1984.

"Look, there are no Jackie Robinsons . . ." Ovid Demaris, *Parade,* January 1, 1984.

"I'm very contra . . ." Nancy Collins, *Rolling Stone,* March 29, 1984.

CHAPTER 2

"The year I remember most vividly . . ." *Jack Nicholson: The Search for a Superstar,* Norman Dickens, Signet, 1975.

"chubby and quite short . . ." *Jack Nicholson: The Search for a Superstar,* Norman Dickens, Signet, 1975.

"He never said he wanted to make it . . ." *Jack Nicholson: The Search for a Superstar*, Norman Dickens, Signet, 1975.

"I got sort of talked into it by a teacher . . ." *Time*, November 30, 1970.

"Well, by the time I had waited a year . . ." *Jack Nicholson: Face to Face*, Richard David Crane and Christopher Fryer, M. Evans and Co., Inc., 1975.

CHAPTER 3
"Harry Dean Stanton, who was one of my close sidekicks . . ." *Playboy*, 1972.

"I would sit on Jack's lap . . ." *Time*, August 12, 1974.

"I've balled everybody . . ." *Newsweek*, December 7, 1970.

"The secret inner pressure about monogamy . . ." *Time*, August 12, 1974.

"My divorce was good like the marriage was . . ." *Jack Nicholson: Face to Face*, Richard David Crane and Christopher Fryer, M. Evans and Co., Inc., 1975.

"He worked hard, but at times . . ." *Jack Nicholson: The Search for a Superstar*, Norman Dickens, Signet, 1975.

"I swear to you . . ." Paul Attanasio, *Washington Post*, June 14, 1985.

"I picked Jack for the lead . . ." *Jack Nicholson: The Search for a Superstar*, Norman Dickens, Signet, 1975.

"I thought, within a few weeks, I'd be a star . . ." *Jack Nicholson: The Search for a Superstar*, Norman Dickens, Signet, 1975.

CHAPTER 4
"The first movies I made are so unbearable . . ." Stephen Schiff, *Vanity Fair*, 1986.

CHAPTER 5
"Not a single other human being . . ." Harry Clein, *Entertainment World*, November 7, 1969.

"I took a full year to do the two pictures . . ." *Jack Nicholson: Face to Face*, Richard David Crane and Christopher Fryer, M. Evans and Co., Inc., 1975.

CHAPTER 6
"The first time I took acid . . ." Joseph Gelmis, *Newsday*, December 17, 1969.

CHAPTER 7
"Terry Southern was brought in . . ." Rex Reed, *New York Times*, March 1, 1970.

"He came to me and said he wanted to do it . . ." *Jack Nicholson: Face to Face*, Richard David Crane and Christopher Fryer, M. Evans and Co., Inc., 1975.

"At this point, Jack . . ." *Jack Nicholson: Face to Face*, Richard David Crane and Christopher Fryer, M. Evans and Co., Inc., 1975.

"[It] all worked out great . . ." Harry Clein, *Entertainment World*, November 7, 1969.

"I wanted to use a real Texan . . ." *Jack Nicholson: Face to Face*, Richard David Crane and Christopher Fryer, M. Evans and Co., Inc., 1975.

"Each time I did a take or an angle . . ." *Playboy*, 1972.

"If you read that character in the script . . ." Joseph Gelmis, *Newsday*, December 17, 1969.

"He really is a patriot . . ." Paul Attanasio, *Washington Post*, June 14, 1985.

"I got myself locked right into the sociological . . ." *The Films of Jack Nicholson*, Douglas Brode, Citadel Press, 1987.

"Oh, babe, I could do a bike picture'd . . ." Stephen Schiff, *Vanity Fair*, August 1986.

CHAPTER 8
"I've already overscheduled my work . . ." Rex Reed, *New York Times*, March 1, 1970.

"[It was] just me and him in the room . . ." Rex Reed, *New York Times*, March 1, 1970.

"I like to finish what I start . . ." Rex Reed, *New York Times*, March 1, 1970.

"Years ago, when I was maybe twenty . . ." *Jack Nicholson: The Search for a Superstar*, Norman Dickens, Signet, 1975.

CHAPTER 9
"She says that all the time . . ." Nancy Collins, *Rolling Stone*, March 29, 1984.

"If the world were an island . . ." *Jack Nicholson: The Search for a Superstar*, Norman Dickens, Signet, 1975.

"I think he'd like for Michelle and him . . ." *Jack Nicholson: Face to Face,* Richard David Crane and Christopher Fryer, M. Evans and Co., Inc., 1975.

"First of all, on one level . . ." *Jack Nicholson: Face to Face*, Richard David Crane and Christopher Fryer, M. Evans and Co., Inc., 1975.

"He brags about . . ." *Jack Nicholson: Face to Face,* Richard David Crane and Christopher Fryer, M. Evans and Co., Inc., 1975.

CHAPTER 10
"There is James Cagney . . ." Ron Rosenbaum, *New York Times Magazine*, July 13, 1986.

"[Jack] did me this huge favor . . ." *Jack Nicholson: Face to Face,* Richard David Crane and Christopher Fryer, M. Evans and Co., Inc., 1975.

CHAPTER 11
"Buddusky is killed . . ." *The Films of Jack Nicholson,* Douglas Brode, Citadel Press, 1987.

CHAPTER 12
"One of the secrets of *Chinatown* . . ." Ron Rosenbaum, *New York Times Magazine,* July 13, 1986.

"The only time that Anjelica came to visit . . ." *The Hustons,* Lawrence Grobel, Charles Scribner's Sons, 1989.

"Jack wanted a lot of money . . ." *Jack Nicholson: Face to Face,* Richard David Crane and Christopher Fryer, M. Evans and Co., Inc., 1975.

"I suppose I *might* have put . . ." Deborah Caulfield, *Los Angeles Times,* June 16, 1985.

CHAPTER 13
"The starting problem with *Cuckoo's Nest* . . ." Helen Dudar, *New York Post,* June 2, 1975.

"I can't tell you the actresses . . ." Evelyn Renold, *Newsday,* January 18, 1976.

"This guy's a scamp . . ." Ron Rosenbaum, *New York Times Magazine,* July 13, 1986.

CHAPTER 14
"I didn't blame her in the beginning . . ." Nancy Collins, *Rolling Stone,* March 29, 1984.

"When I heard about . . ." Nancy Collins, *Rolling Stone,* March 29, 1984.

"If you told me twenty years ago . . ." Nancy Collins, *Rolling Stone,* March 29, 1984.

"I was up very early . . ." *The Films of Jack Nicholson*, Douglas Brode, Citadel Press, 1987.

"It's grueling work . . ." Mary Rourke, *Women's Wear Daily*, November 11, 1977.

"I used everyone from Gabby Hayes . . ." Mary Rourke, *Women's Wear Daily*, November 11, 1977.

"All men love to play cowboy . . ." Mary Rourke, *Women's Wear Daily*, November 11, 1977.

CHAPTER 15

"Within the next six months . . ." *The Films of Jack Nicholson*, Douglas Brode, Citadel Press, 1987.

"Grand Guignol was the story's . . ." Lewis Archibald, *The Aquarian*, November 30, 1983.

"[Jack] would lurch into the house . . ." Peter Lester, *People*, July 28, 1980.

CHAPTER 16

"I'm drawn to the sensual area of acting . . ." Seth Cagin, *Soho Weekly News*, March 25, 1981.

"I have rarely spoken to anyone . . ." Arthur Bell, *The Village Voice*, March 18, 1981.

"This is a particular kind of love story . . ." Carol Olten, *San Diego Union*, March 15, 1981.

"Whereas that character has been played . . ." Lewis Archibald, *The Aquarian*, November 30, 1983.

"She was the great gift . . ." Arthur Bell, *The Village Voice*, March 18, 1981.

"Doing it on-screen has to be real . . ." Nancy Collins, *Rolling Stone*, March 29, 1984.

"I wanted to do an action movie . . ." Wayne Robins, *Newsday*, February 5, 1982.

"It's one of the most physically demanding . . ." Wayne Robins, *Newsday,* February 5, 1982.

"I always had this horrible feeling . . ." Jeffrey Wells, *New York Post,* February 2, 1982.

CHAPTER 17
"You know, *Easy Rider* was the part . . ." Lewis Archibald, *The Aquarian,* November 30, 1983.

"There is something actorish . . ." Nancy Collins, *Rolling Stone,* March 29, 1984.

"I love being praised . . ." Wayne Robins, *Newsday,* February 5, 1982.

"extremely productive, creatively adventurous . . ." Nancy Collins, *Rolling Stone,* March 29, 1984.

"principally because I thought . . ." Lewis Archibald, *The Aquarian,* November 30, 1983.

CHAPTER 18
"I honestly didn't understand it . . ." Wayne Robins, *Newsday,* February 5, 1982.

"I think he's the current king of the world . . ." Rosemary Breslin, *New York Daily News,* June 9, 1985.

"It seems to me, Jack . . ." Ron Rosenbaum, *New York Times Magazine,* July 13, 1986.

"I didn't have to gain weight . . ." Janet Maslin, *New York Times,* June 9, 1985.

CHAPTER 19
"realized he is like a two-hundred-year-old child . . ." *The Films of Jack Nicholson,* Douglas Brode, Citadel Press, 1987.

"We were all Jack's girls . . ." *The Films of Jack Nicholson,* Douglas Brode, Citadel Press, 1987.

CHAPTER 20
"We thought, 'Well, Willem Dafoe . . .'" Stephen Rebello, *Cinefantastique*, November 1989.

"Because Jack Nicholson is such a strong . . ." *Batman: The Official Book of the Movie*, John Marriott, Bantam Books, 1989.

"[Jack would] always question . . ." *Cinefantastique*, November 1989.

"Every actor always worries . . ." Joe Morgenstern, *GQ*, January 1990.

"short-wired . . ." Aljean Harmetz, *New York Times*, June 18, 1989.

"You know, Jack's role . . ." Hilary de Vries, *New York Times*, February 5, 1989.

CHAPTER 21
"These were two of my oldest friends . . ." Janet Maslin, *New York Times*, June 9, 1985.

"I'm flat about twenty-five percent more of the time . . ." Aljean Harmetz, *New York Times Magazine*, September 10, 1989.

"I'm not Roman Polanski . . ." Charles Champlin, *Empire*, September 1989.

CHAPTER 22
"their relationship had become . . ." Kenelm Jenour, *Playboy*, December 1989.

"absolutely lost without Anjelica . . ." Tony Castro and Paul Francis, *Globe*, August 7, 1990.

About the Authors

Barbara and Scott Siegel are the authors of thirty-seven books, including Avon's recently published trade paperback edition of *The Encyclopedia of Hollywood*, which movie critic Kathleen Carroll of the *New York Daily News* called "A treasure trove of juicy information," and which movie critic Jeff Strickler of the *Minneapolis Star Tribune* described as "One of the most impressive film reference books I've seen . . . It's destined to become one of the most-useful and most-used Hollywood reference texts." They are also the authors of *The Celebrity Phone Book*, an A-Z guide to the addresses and phone numbers of more than 4,250 famous people.

The two Siegels live in Gotham, which is hardly A Safe Place, and even worse than that, a veritable Cuckoo's Nest. However, they have a consuming love for the restaurants in Chinatown (in spite of occasional Heartburn). Their *all*-consuming love, though, is for each other—a thought dangerously close to The Border of sentiment and, therefore, The Last Detail of their biography.

The Best in Biographies from Avon Books

IT'S ALWAYS SOMETHING
by Gilda Radner 71072-2/$5.95 US/$6.95 Can

ALMOST GOLDEN: JESSICA SAVITCH AND THE SELLING OF TELEVISION NEWS
by Gwenda Blair 70752-7/$4.50 US/$5.95 Can

CARY GRANT: THE LONELY HEART
by Charles Higham and Roy Moseley
71099-9/$4.95 US/$5.95 Can

I, TINA
by Tina Turner with Kurt Loder
70097-2/$4.95 US/$5.95 Can

ONE MORE TIME
by Carol Burnett 70449-8/$4.95 US/$5.95 Can

PATTY HEARST: HER OWN STORY
by Patricia Campbell Hearst with Alvin Moscow
70651-2/$4.50 US/$5.95 Can

PICASSO: CREATOR AND DESTROYER
by Arianna Stassinopoulos Huffington
70755-1/$4.95 US/$5.95 Can

WINFIELD: A PLAYER'S LIFE
by Dave Winfield with Tom Parker
70709-9/$4.50 US/$5.50 Can

THE PHENOMENAL
NATIONAL BESTSELLERS
FROM TRACY KIDDER

A·M·O·N·G
SCHOOLCHILDREN

71089-7/$9.95 US/$11.95 Can

For an entire year Tracy Kidder lived among twenty school-children and their indomitable, compassionate teacher—sharing their joys, their catastrophes, and their small but essential triumphs.

THE SOUL
OF A NEW MACHINE

71115-X/$9.95 US/$11.95 Can

Tracy Kidder's "true life-adventure is the story of Data General Corporation's race to design and build the Eagle, a brand new 32-bit supermini computer, in the course of just a year and a half...compelling entertainment."

Washington Post Book World

HOUSE

71114-1/$9.95 US/$11.95 Can

With all the excitement and drama of a great novel, Kidder now takes us to the heart of the American dream—into the intimate lives of a family building their first house.